On
Imperialist
Globalization

FIDEL CASTRO
On Imperialist Globalization
Two Speeches

Zed Books
London and New York

Fidel Castro on Imperialist Globalization
was first published by LeftWord Books in India in 1999.

Published in the rest of the world by
Zed Books Ltd, 7 Cynthia Street, London N1 9JF, UK and
Room 400, 175 Fifth Avenue, New York, NY10010, USA in 2002.

Distributed in the USA exclusively by
Palgrave, a division of St Martin's Press
LLC, 175 Fifth Avenue, NY 10010, USA.

A catalogue record for this book is available from the British Library.

Library of Congress Cataloging-in-Publication Data has been applied for.

ISBN 1 84277 268 6 hb
ISBN 1 84277 269 4 pb

Fidel Castro has
been applying his formidable intellectual powers and revolutionary
experience in the recent period to analyse the phenomenon of neo-liberal
globalization. Piercing the veil of the global propaganda of imperialism,
Fidel Castro, in a series of major public speeches, has bared the inner
workings of the financial and economic system dominated by the United
States. Since Cuba has been a special target of the imperialist offensive in
the nineties, Castro is able to draw upon his unique experience of leading
a small socialist country which is challenging the imperialist might, resolute
in defending the socialist system created by the endeavours of the Cuban
people.

The two speeches published here were both delivered in 1999,
The first is the Master Lecture delivered at the University of Venezuela,
Caracas, in February. It is one of the most memorable speeches from a
masterly orator who has made a number of great speeches. For four and a
half hours, Castro expounded on the meaning of neo-liberal globalization,
holding an audience of mostly young people spellbound. Later he summed
up what the speech meant:

'I expressed my essential ideas. In summary: what I think about neo-liberal globalization and how absolutely unsustainable the economic order imposed on humankind is, both socially and environmentally. . . . A special emphasis was made on the significance of ideas and the demoralization and uncertainty of neo-liberal theoreticians. The strategies and tactics for struggle, probable course of events and our full confidence in man's ability to survive were also analyzed.'

Castro spoke at the same venue where he had spoken exactly 40 years before, in 1959, fresh from the triumph of the Cuban revolution. The range of the speech published here is breathtaking. Fidel unfolds, with eloquent clarity, the mechanisms of exploitation, the US Federal Reserve, the Bretton Woods institutions, the World Trade Organization, the transnational corporations, the culture industry which manufactures synthetic dreams. He exposes a system which imposes a high infant mortality rate in Bronx, New York and thrives on sweated labour of women and children in South America. The speech is suffused with the revolutionary experience of Cuba. The speech concludes with revolutionary insights into the future course of the struggle against an unsustainable order.

The second speech was delivered at the closing ceremony of the first International Congress on Culture and Development, held in Havana in June 1999. The speech complements the themes expounded at the Master Lecture at Caracas. Here the focus shifts to the onslaughts on sovereignty by the triumphalist imperialist order dominated by a sole superpower. Along with the attacks on culture through its subjugation to a system operated by transnational corporations who monopolize the communication industry, the speech gives a detailed exposition of the NATO aggression in Yugoslavia. The facts about Yugoslavia obscured by imperialist rewriting of history are brilliantly exposed. Fidel argues that culture and sovereignty are inter-related and the defence of both against the depredations of a rapacious market provide the framework for the assertion that national sovereignty cannot be surrendered to a self-serving imperial order.

Fidel Castro's powerful speeches give voice to the worldwide opposition gathering against the spurious consensus purveyed about the neo-liberal global order. This book hopefully will contribute to the alternative vision still in the making.

Publisher

A REVOLUTION
CAN ONLY BE BORN
FROM CULTURE AND IDEAS

I do not
have a written speech, unfortunately, but I brought some notes that I
thought would be useful for the sake of precision. Still I have realized that
a booklet is missing, one that I had read, underlined, noted with great care
and then . . . left at my hotel. I have sent for it, and I hope they find it
because this copy here is not underlined.

At least I should address this audience formally, shouldn't I? I
am not going to make a long list of the many excellent friends we have
here. [*Someone in the audience says, 'We cannot hear'.*] Listen, I do not
have that much voice and if I start shouting . . . I thought there were better
microphones here.

How many of you cannot hear over there? Please, raise you hands.
If someone does not fix this, we can invite you to sit around here or some
place where you can hear.

I am going to try to get closer to this small microphone, right?
But allow me to begin properly.

Dear friends,

I was going to say that today, February 3, 1999, it is 40 years and 10 days to this day that I first visited this university and we met in this same place. Of course, you understand that I am moved – without the melodrama you find in certain soap operas at the moment – as it would have been unimaginable then that one day, so many years later, I would return to this place.

Several weeks ago, on January 1st, 1999, on the occasion of the fortieth anniversary of the triumph of the Revolution, I stood on the same balcony where I had spoken on January 1st, 1959 in Santiago de Cuba. I was reflecting with the audience gathered there that the people of today are not the same people who were there at the time because of the 11 million Cubans we are today, 7,190,000 were born after that date. I said that they were two different people and yet, one and the same eternal people of Cuba.

I also reminded them that the immense majority of those who were 50 years old then are no longer alive, and that those who were children at that time are over 40 today.

socialism? no, no, no

So many changes, so many differences, and how special it was for us to think that there was the people that had started a profound revolution when they were practically illiterate, when 30 per cent of adults could not read or write and perhaps an additional 50 per cent had not reached fifth grade. We estimated that with a population of almost 7 million, possibly little over 150,000 people had gone beyond fifth grade while today the university graduates alone amount to 600,000, and there are almost 300,000 teachers and professors.

I told my fellow countrymen – in paying tribute to the people who had achieved that first great triumph 40 years ago – that in spite of an enormous educational backwardness, they had been able to undertake and defend an extraordinary revolutionary feat. Something else: probably their political culture was lower than their educational level.

Those were times of brutal anti-communism, the final years of McCarthyism, when by all possible means our powerful and imperial neighbour had tried to sow in the minds of our noble people all possible lies and prejudices. Oftentimes, I would meet a common citizen and ask him a number of questions: whether he believed we should undertake a land reform; whether it would be fair for families to own the homes for which at times they paid big landlords almost half their salaries. Also, if he believed that it was right that all those banks where the people's money was deposited should be owned by the people in order to finance with those resources the development of the country instead of being owned by private institutions. Whether those big factories – most of them foreign-owned – should belong to, and produce for, the people . . . things like that. I could ask ten, fifteen similar questions and he would agree absolutely: 'Yes, it would be great.'

In essence, if all those big stores and all those profitable businesses that only enriched their privileged owners belonged to the people and were used to enrich the people, would you agree? 'Yes, yes', he would answer immediately. He agreed completely with each of these simple proposals. So, then I asked him: Would you agree with socialism? Answer: 'Socialism? No, no, no, not with socialism.' Let alone communism . . . There was so much prejudice that this was an even more scaring word.

Revolutionary legislation was what contributed the most to creating a socialist consciousness in our people. Then, it was that very people – illiterate or semi-illiterate at the beginning – who had to start by teaching many of its children to read and write. The same people that out of love for liberty and yearning for justice had overthrown the tyranny and carried out, and heroically defended, the most profound social revolution in this hemisphere.

In 1961, only two years after the triumph, with the support of young students working as teachers, about 1 million people learned how to read and write. They went to the countryside, to the mountains, the remotest places and there they taught people that were even 80 years old how to read and write. Later on, there were follow-up courses and the necessary steps were taken in a constant effort to attain what we have today. A revolution can only be born from culture and ideas.

No people become revolutionary by force. Those who sow ideas have no need to suppress the people ever. Weapons in the hands of that same people are used to fight those abroad who try to take away their achievements.

Forgive me for touching on this issue because I did not come here to preach socialism or communism and I do not want to be misinterpreted. Nor did I come here to propose radical legislation or anything of the sort. I was simply reflecting on our experience that showed us the importance of ideas, the importance of believing in man, the importance of trusting the people. This is extremely important when mankind is facing such complicated and difficult times.

a united people, a people armed with just ideas

Naturally, on January 1st this year in Santiago de Cuba it was fitting to acknowledge, in a very special way, that that Revolution which had managed to survive 40 years and mark this anniversary without folding its banners, without surrendering, was mainly the work of the people gathered there, young people and mature men and women. They had received their education under the Revolution and were capable of that feat, thus writing pages of noble and well-earned glory for our nation and our brothers and sisters in the Americas.

We could say that thanks to the efforts of three generations of Cubans, *vis-à-vis* the mightiest power, the biggest empire ever in man's history, this sort of miracle came true: that a small country would undergo such an ordeal and achieve victory.

Our even greater recognition went to those countrymen who in the past 10 years – the latest 8 years, to be precise – had been willing to withstand the double blockade resulting from the collapse of the socialist camp and the demise of the USSR which left our neighbour as the sole superpower in a unipolar world, unrivalled in the political, economic, military, technological and cultural fields. I do not mean the value of their culture but rather the tremendous power they exercise to impose their culture on the rest of the world.

However, it was unable to defeat a united people, a people armed with just ideas, a people endowed with a great political consciousness because that is most important for us. We have resisted everything and are ready to continue resisting for as long as need be thanks to the seeds planted throughout those decades, thanks to the ideas and the consciousness developed during that time.

It has been our best weapon and it shall remain so, even in nuclear times. Now that I mention it, we even had experiences related to that type of weapons because at a given moment, who knows how many bombs and how many nuclear missiles were aimed at our small island during the well-known Missile Crisis in October 1962. Even in times of smart weapons – which sometimes make mistakes and strike 100 or 200 km. away from their targets but which have a certain degree of precision – man's intelligence will always be greater than any of these sophisticated weapons.

The type of fight becomes a matter of concepts. The defence doctrine of our nation, which feels stronger today as it has perfected these concepts, is based on the conclusion that at the end – the end of our invaders – it would be a body combat, a man-to-man and a woman-to-invader combat, whether man or woman.

We have had to wage, and will have to continue waging, a more difficult battle against that extremely powerful empire: a ceaseless ideological battle that they stepped up with all their resources after the collapse of the socialist camp when fully confident in our ideas we decided to continue forward. More than that, to continue forward alone; and when I say alone I am thinking of state entities, without ever forgetting the immense and invincible support and solidarity of the peoples which we always had and which makes us feel under a greater obligation to struggle.

We have accomplished honorable internationalist missions. Over 500,000 Cubans have taken part in such hard and difficult missions. The children of that people which could not read or write developed such a high consciousness that they shed their sweat, and even their blood, for other peoples; in short, for any people in the world.

When the special period began we said: 'Now, our first internationalist duty is to defend this bulwark'. We meant what Martí had described in the last words he wrote the day before his death, when he said that the main objective of his struggle had to go undeclared in order to be accomplished. Martí, who was not only a true believer in his ideas but also a wholehearted follower of Bolívar's, had set himself an objective. According to his own words, it was to 'timely prevent with the independence of Cuba that the United States should expand itself over the Antilles and fall, with this additional might, on our lands in the Americas. Everything I have done up so far, and everything I will do, is for this purpose.'

It was his political will and he expressed his life's aspiration: to prevent the fall of that first trench which the northern neighbours had so many times tried to occupy. That trench is still there, and will continue to be there, with a people willing to fight to death to prevent the fall of that trench of the Americas. The people there is capable of defending even the last trench, and whoever defends the last trench and prevents anyone from taking it begins, at that very moment, to attain victory.

Comrades, if you allow me to call you that. That is what we are at this moment and I also believe that here, at this moment, we are defending a trench. And trenches of ideas – forgive me for quoting Martí again – are worth, as he said, more than trenches of stones.

We must discuss ideas here, and so I go back to what I was saying. Many things have happened in these 40 years but the most transcendental is that the world has changed. This world of today in which I am talking to you – to those who had not been born then, and many were far from being born at the time – does not resemble the world of those days.

I tried to find a newspaper where there might be a note on that rally at the university. Fortunately, we do have the complete text of the speech delivered at Plaza del Silencio. The revolutionary fever we had come down with from the mountains only a few days before accompanied us when speaking of revolutionary processes in Latin America and focusing on the liberation of the Dominican people from Trujillo's clutches. I believe that issue took most of the time – or a good part of the time of that meeting – with a tremendous enthusiasm shared by all.

Today, that would not be an issue. Today, there is not one particular people to liberate. Today, there is not one particular people to save. Today, a whole world, all of mankind needs to be liberated and saved. And it is not our task, it is *your* task.

There was not a unipolar world at that time, a single, hegemonistic superpower. Today, the world and all mankind are under the domination of an enormous superpower. Nonetheless, we are convinced that we will win the battle without panglossian optimism – I believe that is a word writers sometimes use. I believe so because you can be sure that if you drop this notebook it will fall in a second, that if this table were not here, this notebook would be on the floor. And the table on which this mighty superpower ruling a unipolar world is objectively standing, is disappearing.

These are objective reasons, and I am sure mankind will provide all the indispensable subjective ones. For this, neither nuclear weapons nor big wars are necessary but ideas. This I say on behalf of that small country we mentioned before, which has struggled staunchly and unhesitatingly for 40 years.

You were saying, calling – to my embarrassment – the name by which I am known, I mean 'Fidel', because I do not have any other title actually. I understand that protocol demands the use of 'His Excellency the President' and so on and so forth. When I heard you chanting: 'Fidel! Fidel! What is it with Fidel that Americans cannot put him down?' I had an idea. So I turned to my neighbour on the right, I mean on the right in terms of geography. There are some people making signs I do not understand, but I say that all of us are in the same combat unit. So, I said to him: well, actually what they should be asking is: 'What is it with the Americans that cannot put him down?' And, that instead of saying 'him' when asking: 'What is it with the Americans that cannot put him down?' They could say: 'What is with the Americans that cannot put Cuba down?' it would be more accurate. I realize words are used to symbolize ideas. That is the way I have always understood it. I never take credit, nor can I take credit, for that myself. [*Exclamations of 'Long Live Fidel!'*]

Yes, we all hope to live long, all of us! In the ideas that we believe and in the conviction that those following in our steps will carry them forward. However, your task – it should be said – will be more difficult than ours.

we, the revolutionaries, have discovered an even more powerful weapon: man thinks and feels

I was saying that we are living in a very different world. This is the first thing we need to understand; then, I was explaining certain political characteristics. Furthermore, the world is globalized, really globalized, a world dominated by the ideology, the standards and the principles of neo-liberal globalization.

In our view, globalization is nobody's whim; it is not even anybody's invention. Globalization is a law of history. It is a consequence of the development of the productive forces – excuse me, please, for using this phrase which might still scare some due to its authorship – it is a consequence of scientific and technologic development, so much so that even the author of this phrase, Karl Marx, who had great confidence in human talent, possibly was unable to imagine it.

Certain other things remind me of some of the basic ideas of that thinker among great thinkers. It comes to one's mind that even what he conceived as an ideal for human society could never come true – and this is increasingly clear – if it was not in a globalized world. Not for a second did he think that in the tiny island of Cuba – just to give you an example – a socialist society, or the building of socialism would be attempted, least of all so near to such a powerful capitalist neighbour.

But, yes, we have tried. Furthermore, we made it and we have defended it. And we have also known 40 years of blockade, threats, aggression, and sufferings.

Today, since we are the only ones, all the propaganda, all the mass media mastering the world are used by the United States in the ideological and political warfare against our revolutionary process in the same way as it uses its immense power in all fields – mainly the economic – and its international political influence in the economic warfare against Cuba.

We say 'blockade', but blockade does not mean much. I wish it were an economic blockade! What our country has been enduring for a long time is true economic warfare. Do you want evidence? You can go anywhere in the world, any factory owned by an American company, to buy a cap or a kerchief to export to Cuba. Even if produced by nationals of the country in question with raw materials originated in the same country, the United States government thousands of miles away, bans the sale of such a cap or kerchief. Is that blockade or economic warfare?

Do you want an additional example? If by any chance one of you wins the lottery – I do not know if you have lottery here – or finds a treasure, that is possible, and decides to build a small factory in Cuba, you can be sure of receiving very soon the visit of a senior American diplomat, perhaps even the ambassador himself. He will try to persuade you, put pressure or threaten you with reprisals so that you do not invest your little treasure in a small factory in Cuba. Is it blockade or economic warfare?

Neither does it allow the sale of medicine to Cuba, even if that medicine is indispensable to save a life, and we have had many examples of such cases.

We have withstood that warfare and like in all battles – whether military, political or ideological – there are casualties. There are those who may be confused, some really are, softened or weakened by a combination of economic difficulties, material hardships, the parading of luxury in consumer societies and the nicely sweetened but rotten ideas about the fabulous advantages of their economic system, based on the mean notion that man is an animal moved only by a carrot or when beaten with a whip. We might say that their whole ideological strategy is based on this.

There are casualties, but also, like in all battles and struggles, other people gain experience, fighters become veterans, multiply their qualities and help preserve and increase the morale and strength needed to continue fighting.

We are winning the battle of ideas. Still, the battlefield is not limited to our small island, although the small island has to fight. Today, the world is the battlefield; it is everywhere, in all continents, in all institutions, in every forum. This is the good side of the globalized struggle. We must defend the small island while fighting throughout the huge world they dominate or try to dominate. In many fields they dominate it almost exclusively but not in all fields, nor in the same way, nor in absolutely every country.

They have discovered very intelligent weapons but we, the revolutionaries, have discovered an even more powerful weapon: man thinks and feels. We have learned that around the world, in the countless internationalist missions we have discharged in one field or another throughout the world. Suffice it to mention a single figure: 26,000 Cuban doctors have taken part in them.

The country that was left with only 3,000 out of the 6,000 doctors it had at the triumph of the Revolution, many of them unemployed, but always wanting to migrate to obtain such and such income and salaries. The Revolution has been able to multiply those 3,000 who stayed by training more and more doctors from those who began studying first or second grade in the schools immediately established throughout the country after the Revolution. These people have such a spirit of sacrifice and solidarity that 26,000 of them have accomplished internationalist missions just as other hundreds of thousands Cubans have worked as professionals, teachers, constructors and combatants. Yes, combatants, and we take pride in saying this because fighting against the fascist and racist soldiers of apartheid and contributing to the victory of African peoples to whom that system was the greatest insult is, and will forever be, a reason to feel proud.

But in this ignored – highly ignored – effort we have learned a lot from peoples. We have come to know those peoples and their extraordinary qualities. Among other things we have learned, not only through abstract notions but also in ordinary everyday life, that all men may not be equal in their features but all men are equal in their talents, feelings and other virtues. This proves that, in terms of moral, social, intellectual and human abilities, all men are genetically equal.

Many have made the big mistake of taking themselves for a superior race.

I was saying that life has taught us many things, and this is what nurtures our faith in the people, our faith in man. We did not read this in a little book, we have lived through it; we have had the privilege of living through it.

I have elabourated a bit on these first ideas because of the lost booklet and the microphone problems so I will have to be briefer on other topics. Yes, I should to be briefer, among other things, for personal reasons. Later, I will have to revisit what I said here, check if a comma or a dot are missing, if any data was wrong. I can assure you that for every hour of speech – which may seem easy – two and three hours of revision are needed, going over it once again. A word might be missing. I never remove an idea I have expressed but at times I have to complete it or add a supplementary concept because oral language differs from written language. If I point out to my neighbour, whoever reads it in a paper does not understand anything, or almost anything. Written language only has exclamation and quotation marks while the tone, the hands, the soul you put into things cannot be put in writing.

I realized this difference and now we take good care in transcribing and reviewing papers because the issues we discuss can be important, objectively speaking. Besides, one needs to be extremely careful with a great number of things you cannot even think of.

At a given moment, while I was thinking of the rally I was going to have with you at 5 p.m., I asked myself: what am I going to tell the students? I cannot mention any names, with few exceptions. I can hardly mention any country because at times when I say something in the best of intentions to illustrate an idea I run the risk of being immediately misquoted and then broadcast throughout the world creating a lot of diplomatic problems. And since we have to work together in this global struggle, we cannot make it easy for the enemy and its well-designed and efficient propaganda mechanisms to carry out their permanent work of planting confusion and misinformation. They have done a lot already, but not enough, you see? I have to limit myself a lot for these reasons and I apologize for it.

with their money and technologies they will start buying everything

There is no need here for an extensive explanation on what neo-liberalism is all about. How can I summarize it? Well, I would say this, for instance: neo-liberal globalization wants to turn all countries, especially all our countries, into private property.

What will be left for us of their enormous resources? Because they have accumulated an immense wealth not only looting and exploiting the world but also working the miracle alchemists longed for in the Middle Ages: turning paper into gold. At the same time, they have turned gold into paper and with it they buy everything, everything but souls – more accurately said – everything but the overwhelming majority of souls. They buy natural resources, factories, whole communication systems, services, and so on. They are buying even land around the world assuming that being cheaper than in their own countries it is a good investment for the future.

I wonder: what is it they are going to leave us after turning us practically into second class citizens – pariahs would be a more precise term – in our own countries? They want to turn the world into a huge free-trade zone, it might be more clearly understood this way because, what is a free-trade zone? It is a place with special characteristics where taxes are not paid; where raw materials, spare parts and components are brought in and assembled or various goods produced, especially in labour-intensive sectors. At times, they pay not more than 5 per cent of the salary they must pay in their own countries and the only thing they leave us with are these meagre salaries.

Sadder still: I have seen how they have put many of our countries to compete with one another by favouring those who offer more advantages and tax exemptions to investments. They have put many Third World countries to compete with one another for investments and free-trade zones.

There are countries – I know them – enduring such poverty and unemployment that they have had to establish dozens of free-trade zones as an option within the established world order. It is this, or not having even free-trade zone factories and jobs with certain salaries, even if these amount to only 7 per cent, 6 per cent, 5 per cent or less of the salaries the owners of those factories would have to pay in the countries they come from.

We stated this at the World Trade Organization, in Geneva, several months ago. They want to turn us into a huge free-trade zone, yes, that precisely, then with their money and technologies they will start buying everything. It remains to be seen how many airlines will remain national property, how many shipping lines, how many services will remain the property of the people or the nations.

That is the future we are offered by the neo-liberal globalization. But you should not think that is offered to the workers only. It is also being offered to the national businessmen and to the small and medium-size owners. They will have to compete with the transnational companies' technologies, with their sophisticated equipment, and their world-wide distribution networks; then, look for markets without the substantial trade credits their powerful competitors can use to sell their products.

We in Cuba can have a great factory, let's say a fridge factory. We have one but it is not great and it is far from being the most modern in the world. It suits us well down there, of course, with warm weather raising in the tropics. Let us assume that other Third World countries manufacture fridges of acceptable quality and even at a lower cost. Their powerful competitors constantly renew their designs, invest huge sums of money to lend prestige to their trademarks, manufacture in many free-trade zones paying low wages or anywhere else, tax-free. They also have abundant capital or financial mechanisms for credits that can be repaid in 1, 2 or 3 years, whatever. They dump the market with electric appliances produced in a world riddled with anarchy and chaos in the distribution of investment capital, under the generalized motto of export-based growth and development, as the IMF advises.

What space is there left for national industries? How can they export and to whom? Where are the potential consumers among the billions of poor, hungry and unemployed living in a large part of the globe? Shall we have to wait until all of them can buy a fridge, a TV set, a telephone, an air conditioner, a car, a PC, a house, a garage, fuel and electricity or until they get an unemployment subsidy, market shares and a safe pension? Is that the path leading to development, as they tell us millions of times by all possible means? What will happen to the domestic market if the accelerated reduction of customs barriers – an important source of budget revenues in many Third World countries – is imposed on them?

Neo-liberal theoreticians have been unable to solve, for instance, the serious problem of unemployment in most of the rich countries, let alone the developing countries, and they shall never find a solution under such a ridiculous conception. It is a huge contradiction in the system that the more they invest and resort to technology, the more people are left jobless. Labour productivity and the most sophisticated equipment born out of human talent multiply material wealth as well as poverty and layoffs, what good are they to mankind? Perhaps to help reduce working hours, have more time for resting, leisure, sports, cultural and scientific upgrading? That is impossible because the sacred market laws and competition patterns – increasingly more imaginary than real – in a world of transnationals and megamerges do not allow it at all. Anyway, who are competing and against whom? Monopoly- and merger-oriented giants against giants. There is not a place or a corner in the world for the other alleged players in this competition. For wealthy countries, state-of-the-art industries; for Third World workers, manufacturing jeans, tee-shirts, garments, shoes, planting flowers, exotic fruits and other products increasingly demanded in industrialized societies because they cannot be grown there. We know that in the United States, for instance, they even grow marijuana in greenhouses or in courtyards, and that the value of the marijuana produced in that country is higher than all their corn production although they are the biggest corn producers in the world. In the long run, their laboratories are, or will wind up being, the biggest narcotics producers in the globe, for the time being under the label of sedatives, antidepressants and other types of tablets and products which young people have learned to combine and mix in various ways.

In the happy developed world, though agricultural tasks like picking tomatoes – for which a perfect machine has not yet been invented, a robot capable of picking them according to ripeness, size and other characteristics – cleaning the streets and other unpleasant jobs that nobody wants to do in consumer societies, how do they solve this? Oh! That is what Third World immigrants are for! They themselves do not do that type of work.

For those of us turned foreigners inside our own borders – as I already said – what they leave is the manufacturing of blue jeans and things like that. Under their wonderful economic laws, they make us produce blue jeans as if the world population already was 40 billion and every person had enough money to buy a pair of jeans. I am not criticizing the garment; it is very becoming to young people, more so in the case of young women. No, no, I am not criticizing the garment I am criticizing the jobs they want to leave for us and that has absolutely nothing to do with high technology. So, our universities will become redundant and be left to train low-cost technical staff for the developed world.

You may have read in the press these days that the United States, in view of the needs of their computer, electronic, etc., etc., industries has decided to acquire in the international market – actually the Third World – and grant visas to 200,000 highly-skilled workers for their state-of-the-art industries. You had better be careful because they are looking for trained people. This time it is not to pick tomatoes. They are not very literate, and many people can see this when they confuse Brazil with Bolivia or Bolivia with Brazil, or when surveys show that they do not even know many things about the very United States. They do not even know if a Latin American country they have heard of is in Africa or Europe, and this is not an overstatement. They do not have all the geniuses or highly skilled workers for their state-of-the-art industries, so they come to our world and recruit a few who are then lost for our countries, forever.

Where are the best scientists of our countries, in which laboratories? Which of our countries has laboratories for all the scientists it could train? How much can we pay that scientist and how much can they pay?

Where are they? I know many outstanding Latin Americans who are there. Who trained them? Oh! Venezuela, Guatemala, Brazil, Argentina, any Latin American country did but they have no possibilities in their homeland. Industrialized countries have the monopoly of laboratories and the money. They recruit them and take them away from poor nations. But not only scientists, athletes too. They would like to buy our baseball players the way slaves were sold on one of those stands, I do not remember what they are called...

They are treacherous. Since there is always a soul to be tempted. So says the Bible and that referring to the first human beings that were supposed to be better, right? Because supposedly they were not so wicked nor were they familiar with consumer societies. In those days there was no dollar. All of a sudden, even an athlete who is not absolutely first rate, gets paid a couple of millions, or four, five or six millions, he is given enormous publicity and since Big League batters seem to be so bad, they have some success. I mean no offense for American professional athletes; they are hard working, highly motivated people. Also a commodity bought and sold in the market, although at a high price, but there must be shortcomings in their training because they smuggle in some Cuban pitchers – who, would rank first, second or third – or a shortstop, or a third base. These get there and the pitcher strikes out their best batters and the shortstop does not let a ball go past him.

We would be practically rich if we auctioned Cuban baseball players. They no longer want to pay American baseball players because those are too expensive. They have organized academies in our countries to train players at a very low cost and pay them lower salaries, but still a salary of millions of dollars a year. Together with this, all the TV advertising, plus automobiles from here to there and beautiful women from all ethnic groups linked to automobile advertising and the rest of the commercial advertising you see in some tabloids can tempt more than one of our countrymen.

In Cuba we do not spend any newsprint or other resources in such frivolous advertising. The very few times I watch American TV, I can hardly stand it because every three minutes it stops for a commercial, sometimes a man working out on an exercise bike which is the most boring thing in the world . . . I am not saying it is wrong, I say it is boring. Any programme, even soap operas are interrupted in their sweetest moments of love . . .

In Cuba we buy some soap operas from abroad because we have not been able to cover our needs and some made in Latin American countries are so attractive to the Cuban audience that they even cause people to stop working. At times, we also get good films from Latin America but practically everything circulating in the world is sheer Yankee-made, canned culture.

Actually, what little paper we have in our country is used for textbooks and for our few newspapers with few pages. We cannot use resources to print those glossy magazines – I do not know what they are called – with many pictures, read by beggars in any street of our capitals, advertising those fancy cars with their beautiful escorts and even a yacht and other things, right? That is how they poison people with propaganda, so that beggars are also cruelly influenced and made to dream of a Heaven – unattainable for them – offered by capitalism.

As I said, in our country we operate differently. Still, they have an influence with the image of a society that is not only alienating and economically unequal and unfair, but also socially and environmentally unsustainable.

I usually say as an example that if the consumer pattern means that in Bangladesh, India, Indonesia, Pakistan or China there may be an automobile in every household . . . I apologize to those present who have one. Apparently there is no other choice, there are many avenues and the distances are long here. I mean no criticism but a warning against a model not applicable in a world that has yet to develop. You will surely understand me because Caracas cannot accommodate many more cars. You know they are going to have to build avenues three of four stories high. I can imagine that if they were to do the same in China, then the 100 million hectares of arable land would have to be transformed into highways, gas stations and parking lots leaving practically no space to grow a single grain of rice.

they have impaired the human mind

The consumption pattern they are imposing on the world is sheer madness, chaotic and absurd.

It is not that I think the world should become a monastery. However, I do believe that the planet has no other choice but to define which are going to be the consumption standards or patterns, both attainable and obtainable, in which mankind should be educated.

Everyday, a lower number of people are reading books. Any why should human beings be deprived, for example, of the pleasure of reading a book, or of many other satisfactions in the field of culture and recreation, not only for the sake of acquiring material wealth but also spiritual richness? I am not thinking about men and women working, as in the times of

Frederick Engels, for 14 or 15 hours a day. I am thinking of men and women working 4 hours a day. If technology so allows it, then why work 8 hours? It is only logical that, as productivity increases, less physical and mental effort will be required; that there be less unemployment and the people have more spare time.

Let us call a free man he who does not need to work all week, Saturdays, Sundays or double shifts included, to make ends meet, dashing at all hours in large cities, rushing to the subway or to take a bus . . . Whom are they going to convince that that is a free man? If computers and automatic machines can work wonders in terms of the generation of material goods and services, then why cannot man benefit from the science that he created with his intelligence for the wellbeing of humanity?

Why must the person endure hunger, unemployment, early death from curable diseases, ignorance, the lack of culture and all sorts of human and social afflictions for exclusively commercial reasons and profits? Why, for the sole interest of an over-privileged and powerful elite operating under frenzied economic laws and institutions which are not, were not, and will not be eternal?

Such is the case of the well-known market laws. The market has become today an object of idolatry, a sacred word pronounced at all hours. Why should this be so when it is possible to generate all the wealth required for meeting reasonable human needs compatible with the preservation of nature and life on our planet? We must ponder and reach our own conclusions. Obviously, it is reasonable for people to have food, health, a roof, clothing and education. Also adequate, rational sustainable and secure transportation means; culture, recreation, a broad variety of options and many more things that could be at the reach of human beings and not, of course, a private jet or a yacht for each of the 9.5 billion who will live on the planet within 50 years.

They have impaired the human mind.

Thank goodness that these things did not happen back in the days of the Garden of Eden or of Noah's Ark in the Old Testament. I can imagine that life was a bit more peaceful then. Even if they did have a flood, we are also the victims of floods, all too frequently. Observe what happened recently in Central America. No one knows for sure if as a result of all the climatic constraints we might end up buying tickets or standing in line to board an ark.

they want to square the circle
it must be awful for them

This is the situation, they have instilled all this in people's minds. They have alienated millions and hundreds of millions of people and made them suffer even more, as those people are unable to meet their basic needs because they do not even have a doctor to see or a school to attend.

I mentioned the anarchic, irrational and chaotic formula imposed by neo-liberalism: the investment of hundreds of billions without rhyme or reason; having tens of millions of workers manufacturing the same things: television sets, computer parts, and clips or chips, whatever they are called . . . an endless number of gadgets, including a large number of cars. Everyone is doing the same thing.

They have doubled the capacity for manufacturing cars. Who will buy these cars? Buyers can be found in Africa, Latin America and in many other parts of the world. Only that they do not have a dime to buy cars nor gas, or to pay for the highways or repair shops, which would ultimately ruin Third World countries even more by squandering the resources needed for social development while further destroying the environment.

By creating unsustainable consumer patterns in industrialized countries and sowing impossible dreams throughout the rest of the world, the developed capitalist system has caused great injury to mankind. It has poisoned the atmosphere and depleted its enormous non-renewable natural resources, which mankind will need in the future. Please, do not believe that I am thinking of an idealistic, impossible, absurd world; I am merely trying to imagine what a real world and a happier person could be like. It would not be necessary to mention a commodity, it suffices to mention a concept: inequality has made more than 80 per cent of the people on the planet unhappy, and this is no more than a concept. Concepts and ideas are required that will make possible a viable world, a sustainable world and a better world.

I find amusing the writings of many theoreticians of neo-liberalism and neo-liberal globalization. Actually, I have little time to go to the cinema, practically never, or to watch videos, however good they may be. I rather amuse myself reading the articles these gentlemen write. I can see their analysts, their wisest and most perceptive commentators, immersed in many a great contradiction, in confusion and even despair; they want to square the circle. It must be awful for them.

I recall that once they showed me a squared figure with two lines on the top like this, one in the middle and another one downwards. The object of the game was to draw over the lines with a pencil without lifting it once. I do not know how much time I lost attempting to do it instead of doing my homework or studying math, languages or other subjects. In my childhood days there were no toys like those invented by the industry to entertain children during school time so that they fail their grades but we used to invent games ourselves in which we lost a lot of time.

But they amuse me and I truly enjoy them, at least, I am grateful to them for that but I am also thankful for what they teach me. And do you know whose articles and analyses humour me the most? Oh, the most conservative, the ones who do not even want to hear about the State, who want no mention of it, whatsoever. Those who want a Central Bank on the Moon so that no human being will dare to lower or raise interest rates. It's unbelievable!

They are the ones who make me happiest because when they say certain things, I ask myself: 'Am I wrong? Could this article not have been written by a left wing extremist, a radical?' But, what is this? After seeing [George] Soros write book after book and the last one . . . yes, I had to read that one too. I had no alternative because I reasoned: 'Well, this man is a theoretician but he is also an academician and, furthermore, he has I do not know exactly how many billion dollars as a result of speculative operations. This man must know all about this, all the mechanisms and the tricks. However, he entitled his book: *Capitalism's Global Crisis*, which is quite something. There he states it with absolute seriousness and apparently with such a conviction that I said to myself: Goodness, it seems that I am not the only madman in this world! Actually, many have expressed similar concerns. I pay more attention to them than to the adversaries of the current World Economic Order.

The leftists want to prove that the system will inevitably collapse. This is only logical since it is their duty and, after all, they are right. However, the others do not want this to happen. They become despondent and write many things when faced with a crisis and all sorts of threats. They are baffled. The least you can say is that they have lost faith in their own doctrines.

a small pin, the smallest of holes and the balloon would deflate

Then, those of us who decided to resist in solitude . . . I do not mean geographical solitude but almost complete solitude in the field of ideas because in the aftermath of these disasters there is a skepticism, which is then multiplied by the expert and powerful propaganda machinery of the empire and its allies. All of this causes many people to feel pessimistic and confused since they do not have all the necessary elements for analyzing circumstances from a historical perspective, and consequently, they lose hope.

Those first days were truly bitter, and even before that, as we watched how many people, here and there, became turncoats – and I am not criticizing anyone but the coats . . . Then, again, things change so quickly! Those illusions are now way behind – as we say in Cuba, and I do not know if you also have this saying here – they lasted less than a candy bar at a schoolyard.

They took to the former Soviet Union their neo-liberal and market recipes, causing destruction, truly incredible destruction, disintegrating nations. They brought about the economic and political dismantling of federations of republics reducing life expectancy in some cases by 14 and 15 years, multiplying infant mortality by three to four times and generating social and economic problems which not even a resurrected Dante would dare to imagine.

It is truly pathetic. Those of us who try to be as well-informed as possible about everything that happens everywhere, and we have no other choice but to be more or less well informed, more or less profoundly, otherwise, we would be disoriented. We have what we think is a quite clear notion of the disasters that the market god and its laws and principles have caused. They, together with the recipes that the International Monetary Fund and other neo-colonizing and re-colonizing institutions have recommended and practically imposed on every country. Even wealthy countries like the Europeans have found it necessary to unite and establish a currency so that experts like Soros do not to bring down even the pound sterling. That is a currency not so long ago reigned as a medium of exchange and was the sword and the symbol of a dominating empire that was the master of the world's reserve currency. All these privileges are now in the hands of the United States while the British had to suffer the humiliation of watching the fall of their pound sterling.

Such was the case of the Spanish peseta, the French franc and the Italian lira; they staked their bets on the immense power of their billions because these speculators are gamblers who play with marked cards. They have all the information, the most prominent economists, Nobel Prize laureates, such as the case of the famous company which was one of the most prestigious in the United States, called the Long Term Capital Management. You will have to excuse my 'excellent' English pronunciation, but I prefer the title in Spanish, and practically everyone knows it by its original name, which has been hispanicized. With a total fund almost 4.5 billion dollars, the company mobilized 120 billion for speculative operations.

The company had two Nobel Prize laureates on its payroll together with the most experienced computer software producers. And there you have it. The illustrious gentlemen made a mistake because so many unusual things are happening that they did not foresee some of them. For instance, the difference between treasury bonds at 30 and 29 years was larger than reasonably expected, immediately all the computers and Nobel Prize laureates decided that they had to straddle. Apparently, they had problems with the crisis that ensued, which they did not anticipate. They thought that they had discovered the miracle of a ceaselessly growing capitalism, without crisis . . . We are fortunate that this did not occur to them two or three thousand years ago! It was fortunate that it took Columbus some years to discover this hemisphere, proving the Earth was round. Also that other economic, social and scientific advances were equally delayed since it was on them that such a system, inseparable from its crises, took root, otherwise there would not be any human beings left on this planet. Perhaps there would be nothing left.

Those from the Long Term, as it is commonly known, made a mistake and lost. It was a disaster and it was necessary to go to their rescue, violating all international, ethical, moral and financial norms that the United States had imposed on the world. The President of the Federal Reserve declared in the Senate that if that fund was not bailed out, there would inevitably be an economic catastrophe, both in the United States and in the rest of the world.

Another question: what kind of economy is that prevailing today where a handful of multi-millionaires can cause an economic catastrophe in the United States and in the world? I do not mean the big ones, not Bill Gates and others like him since Bill Gates' fortune is about fifteen times the initial capital with which Long Term mobilized enormous sums from savers, obtaining loans from over 50 banks. But, oh! The international economy would have collapsed had it not been bailed out. And this was stated by one of the most competent and intelligent persons in the United Sates, the Chairman of the Federal Reserve.

That distinguished gentleman knows more than a thing or two. The problem is that he does not say everything he knows because part of the method consists in a total lack of transparency and strong doses of sedatives in case of panic accompanied by sweet and encouraging words: 'Everything is all right, the economy is running smoothly'. This is the accepted and always applied technique. However, the President of the Federal Reserve had to admit before the US Senate that a catastrophe would have occurred if the Fed had not done what it did.

These are the bases of neo-liberal globalization. Do not worry, you may subtract one or twenty more from their fragile structure. What they have created is unsustainable! However, they have caused anguish for many people throughout the world. They have ruined nations with the International Monetary Fund's formula and continue to impoverish countries. They cannot avoid the ruin of these countries, yet they do not cease to do foolish things and in the stock markets they have inflated the prices of shares and continue to do so *ad infinitum*.

In the US stock markets, more than one third of the families' savings and 50 per cent of the pension funds have been invested in shares. One can imagine the impact of a catastrophe similar to that of 1929, when only 5 per cent of the population had their savings invested in the stock market. Today, they would feel terrified and run in haste. That was what they did in August after the crisis in Russia whose share of the world's gross product is only 2 per cent. That crisis made the Dow Jones, the key index of the New York stock market, fall in one day by more than 500 points; 512 to be exact, causing an enormous commotion.

The truth is that the leaders of this dominating system spend most of their time running around the world, from banks to financial institutions. And when they saw what occurred in Russia, a track and field Olympics ensued. They met with the Council on Foreign Relations in New York. Clinton delivered a speech, stating that recession and not inflation was the real danger. In a matter of days, in practically a few hours, they made a 180 degree shift and instead of increasing interest rates what they actually did was to lower them. On October 5 and 6, all the directors of central banks met in Washington. Speeches were delivered, an undetermined number of criticisms were raised to the Monetary Fund and the so-called measures were adopted to reduce the danger. A few days later the US government met with the G-7, which decided to contribute 90 billion dollars to stop the crisis from extending to Brazil and from there to the rest of South America. They were trying to impede the flames from reaching the over-inflated stock markets of the United States. A small pin, the smallest of holes and the balloon would deflate. These are the risks threatening neo-liberal globalization.

That was what they did. Then some of us, myself included, reflected on it and I said: 'They have resources, they have the possibility to manoeuvre and postpone the great crisis for a time'. They could postpone it but not ultimately avoid it. I reflected on the matter and said: 'Apparently they have succeeded thanks to all the measures adopted or imposed: lowering interest rates; 90 billion dollars to support the Fund which had no funds; the steps taken by Japan to confront the bank crisis; Brazil's announcement of harsh economic measures and the timely statement that the US economy had grown more than expected in the third quarter.'

It seemed that things would hold on. However, only a few days ago, we were again surprised by the news from Brazil on the current economic situation. This truly hurts us very much for reasons connected to this very issue, that is, the effort that our peoples must make to join forces and wage the hard struggle that awaits us. Actually, a destructive crisis in Brazil would have an extremely negative impact on Latin America.

At present, despite everything they did, Brazilians are faced with a complicated economic situation, regardless of the fact that the United States and the international financial institutions used up a large part of their recipes and ammunition. Now, after the first months since the great scare, they are demanding new conditions and seem more indifferent to the fate of Brazil.

As for Russia, they intend to keep it on the brink of an abyss. This is not a small country. It is a very large country with a population of 146 million and thousands of nuclear weapons where a social explosion, an internal conflict or any other event can cause terrible damage.

Yet, these gentlemen who manage the world economy are so insane and reckless that, after ruining a country with their recipes, it does not even occur to them to use some of their own printed paper – because that is precisely what the Treasury bonds are, a refuge for terrified speculators; when faced with any risk, speculators would buy United States Treasury bonds – it does not occur to them to use some of the 90 billion designed for the Fund in the prevention of an economic or political catastrophe in Russia. What occurs to them is to impose a bunch of impossible conditions. They demand that budgets, which are already below the indispensable limit, be cut. They also demand free conversion and immediate payment of high debts; a host of requirements that would deplete the remaining reserves of any country. They refuse to think, they have not learned their lesson. They intend to maintain that country in a precarious situation, at the edge of the sword, with humanitarian assistance, imposing conditions and generating truly serious dangers.

However, the Russian issue has not been solved. A country they impoverished, thanks to their advisors and formulas. Nor have they solved the Brazilian issue, a problem they were so very much interested in solving, since it could affect them very closely. Therefore it seemed to me, for example, that this was the last stronghold of the United States stock markets.

It was a close call. Some of the aforementioned measures stabilized the situation a bit. Once again the sale and purchase of shares was unleashed and once again they are off on a race to outer space, preparing the conditions for an even greater crisis, and relatively soon. No one knows what the consequences for the US economy and its society will be.

It is impossible to imagine what would occur in the event of another 1929. They believe they have done away with the risk of a crisis like that of 1929, and actually they have solved nothing. They have not even been able to prevent the Brazilian crisis consequently, they may affect the whole integration process in South America, the whole integration process in Latin America and the interests of all our countries. That was why I said that recently we had received bad news.

However, there is a cause for everything and an explanation, and after waiting and watching how they think, what they say, what they do one can actually guess what is hidden in their minds. The important thing with those people is not so much to believe what they are saying but, based on what they are saying, to penetrate their brains with the least possible trauma – as we would not want to harm them – to know what they are actually thinking, to know what they have not said and why they have not said it.

This is how they behave. This is also why it is to us a matter of profound interest, a source of reflection, encouragement and reassertion of our convictions. Because we lived through the days of uncertainty and bitterness that I previously described, and witnessed the loss of faith of many progressive men and women. Now, we can see that the truths are gaining ground and that many people are now beginning to think more profoundly. And those who claimed the end of history and the final victory of their anachronistic and selfish concepts are now in decline and in undeniable demoralization.

These past eight years – since 1991, in other words, from the collapse of the USSR to date – have been hard years for us in every sense, in this sense as well, in terms of ideas and conceptions. Now we see that the high and mighty, those who thought they had created a system or an empire that would last one thousand years are beginning to realize that the bases of that system, of that empire, are falling apart.

Mr Nixon came along and the great empire embezzled us all

What is the legacy of this global capitalism or of this neo-liberal capitalist globalization? Not only that capitalism that we know from its very sources, that capitalism from which this one was born which was progressive yesterday but reactionary and unsustainable today. A process many of you, historians, and those who are not like the students of economics must know. A history of 250 to 300 years, whose primary theoretician, Adam Smith, whom you know well, published his book in 1776, the same year of the Declaration of Independence of the United States. He was a great talent, undoubtedly, a great intelligence. I do not think he was a sinner, a culprit or a bandit. He studied the economic system that emerged in Europe while it was in full bloom. He pondered, examined and outlined the theoretical bases of capitalism. The capitalism of his day, because Adam Smith could have never imagined this one.

In those days of small workshops and factories, Adam Smith felt that the individual interest was the prime motivation of economic activity and that its private and competitive quest constituted the basic source of public welfare. It was not necessary to appeal to man's humanity but his love of himself.

Personal property and management were all that was compatible with the small industries' world that Adam Smith knew. He did not even live to see the enormous factories and the impressive masses of workers at the end of the eighteenth century. He could much less imagine the gigantic corporations and modern transnational companies with millions of shares and managed by professional executives who have nothing to do with the ownership of these entities and whose main function it is to occasionally report to the shareholders. They decide, however, which dividends are paid, how much and where to invest. These forms of property, management and enjoyment of the wealth produced have nothing to do with the world he lived in.

Nevertheless, the system continued to develop and gained considerable momentum during the English Industrial Revolution. The working class emerged and so did Karl Marx, who in my view, with all due respect to those who may be of a different view, was the greatest economic and political thinker of all times. No one learned more about the laws and principles of the capitalist system than Marx. Presently, more than a few members of the capitalist elite, anguished by the current crisis, are reading Marx, seeking a possible diagnosis and remedy for the evils of today. Socialism, as the antithesis of capitalism, surfaced with Marx.

The struggle between those ideas symbolized by both men of thought has persisted for many years and still continues. The original capitalism continued to develop under the principles of its most prominent theoretician until approximately World War I.

From before the War, a certain level of globalization existed. There was a gold standard for the international monetary system. In 1929, there was the great crisis followed by the great recession that lasted over 10 years. Then, another important thinker emerged, John Maynard Keynes. He is one of the four pillars of economic thought that had an enormous political impact on the last three centuries and the indelible seal of each of his predecessors. Keynes was a man of advanced ideas for his time, not like Karl Marx's, although quite respectful of Marx, and coincided with him in certain concepts. He elaborated the formulas that extricated the United States from the great depression.

Of course, he did not do it alone. A group of scholars agreed with him and were under his influence. At that time, there were practically no economists, nor were they taken very seriously. I do not know if this was for better or for worse, it all depends . . . However, highly trained groups began to surge. They had plenty of statistical information and conducted extensive studies and during the Roosevelt administration in a country that was both exhausted and anguished by endless years of recession; many of them became prominent cabinet members or and so on. Keynes' theories helped pull capitalism out of the worst crisis it had ever known.

There was a temporary suspension of the gold standard that was later re-established by Roosevelt in 1934, if I remember correctly. I do know, however, that it was maintained until 1971. It must have lasted 37 consecutive years until Mr Nixon came along and the great empire embezzled us all.

Perhaps you are rightly wondering why I am talking about this. I have mentioned three characters, although I still have not referred to the fourth one, because it is very important to know the history of the system which currently rules the world; its anatomy, principles, evolution and experiences, in order to understand that this creature, which came into being almost three centuries ago, is reaching its final stage. It is convenient to know this, and it is almost time to perform an autopsy on it before it finally dies, lest that many of us would die with it, or if this takes too long, that all of us would die as well.

I mentioned the gold standard because it had a lot to do with the problems that we are now confronting. Towards the end of World War II, an attempt was made to establish an institution that would regulate and step up world trade. The economic situation was in shambles as a consequence of the long, destructive and bloody war. Therefore, the well-known Bretton Woods Agreement was established by a number of countries, including the most influential and the wealthiest.

The United States was already the richest nation accumulating 80 per cent of the world gold. A fixed exchange currency was established based on gold, the gold-dollar standard so to say, because gold was combined with the US bank note, which then became the international reserve currency. This gave the United States a special privilege and an enormous power, which it has continued to use in its own best interest. It gave that country the power to manipulate the world economy, set rules, and prevail in the International Monetary Fund where 85 per cent of the votes are required to make any decision. So with its 17.5 per cent, the US may obstruct any decision of that institution. Thus, it controls and is practically the owner of the Fund. It has the last say and has been able to impose worldwide the economic order that we suffer today.

However, Nixon cheated before that. Initially the US had 30 billion dollars in gold whose price was maintained through a strict control of the market at 35 dollars – the so-called troy ounce. Soon, it began to incur in tax-free expenditures, tax-free wars. The United States spent more than 500 billion dollars on the Vietnam adventure. By then, they were running out of gold. They only had 10 billion dollars left and, at that pace, they were going to lose it all. In a speech delivered on 17 August 1971, I think, Nixon openly declared that he suspended the US dollar conversion into gold.

As I already explained, they were able to maintain a fixed price for gold thanks to a strict control of the market, the aforementioned 35 dollars an ounce. If there were an excess gold supply in the market they would buy; after all, it did not cost them anything. They would hand over those bank notes and receive gold in exchange, thus avoiding a drop in prices. If an excessive gold demand threatened to raise its price, they would do the opposite. They would sell gold from their abundant reserves, in order to lower its price. Many countries backed their currency with gold reserves or with US bank notes. At least, there was a relatively stable monetary system for trade.

From the moment that Nixon, defrauding the whole world and everyone who owned one of those bills announced that the value of US dollar bills would no longer be received in physical gold he suspended the most sacred commitment undertaken through an international treaty. This is something he did unilaterally, by presidential decree or through some other legal procedure, it was not even a House decision, and the world had hundreds of billions of dollars in the central banks' reserves.

They kept the gold. Later, prices rose. The value of the remaining gold, worth 10 billion dollars, rose to more than the 30 billion dollars they initially had in physical gold. They also kept all privileges of the system, the value of their Treasury bonds and their bank notes that continued to be the compulsory reserve currency in the countries' central banks. In order to get those dollars the countries had to export all their goods, while the United States only had to pay the printing costs. Consequently, the US economic power became even greater, and in exchange, it began to destabilize the world. How? The other currencies suffered fluctuations. Their values changed from day to day. Money speculation was unleashed; speculative sales and purchases of currencies amounting today to colossal sums, based on the constant fluctuation of their values. A new phenomenon had emerged, which is now beyond control.

Currency speculation which only 14 years ago involved 150 billion dollars a year now amounts to more than 1 trillion a day. I would like to point out, so that we may understand each other in this Babel Tower of figures and numbers which often give rise to confusions as well as translation mistakes and misunderstandings, that I am not referring to the term *billón* in Spanish, as there is much confusion between the meaning of *billion* in English and *billón* in Spanish. The former equals one thousand million and the latter one million million. This is what they call a 'trillion' in the United States. A new term has just begun to circulate, the milliard which also represents one thousand million. I said, and I repeat, in order to avoid any confusion, that the currency speculative operations reached a figure of more than a million million dollars a day, that is, one trillion.

It has grown by two thousand times in 14 years as a result of the measures adopted by the United States in 1971 which caused the fluctuation of all the currencies, either within certain limits or freely. Consequently, we now have this new capitalism, something which would have never occurred to Adam Smith, not even in his worst nightmares when he wrote his book on the wealth of nations.

Other new and equally uncontrollable phenomena have emerged – I already mentioned one – the hedge funds. In fact, there are hundreds or thousands of these. Think of what might be happening, and what the repercussions might be, after the Chairman of the US Federal Reserve declared that one of them might have caused an economic cataclysm in the United States and the rest of the world. He is well informed. He should know in detail what is truly happening.

One can guess, judging by certain articles published in a number of conservative magazines because they know. At times, they need to print something that will support their arguments. However, they try to be extremely discreet. But there are no longer so many foolish people in the world and it is not hard to discern what they did not want to say. A phrase published in a very famous British magazine criticizing the measures adopted by Greenspan in connection with the well-known hedge fund said more or less that perhaps Greenspan had additional information. I cannot exactly recall the phrase used which was more subtle.

However, it is possible to discern from this magazine, which is careful about what it prints and is a highly specialized journal that it knew more than it was saying. And although it did not agree with the decision of the Chairman of the Reserve, it knew perfectly well what he meant when he ascertained that 'it is necessary to save this Fund'. Undoubtedly, both the magazine and Greenspan knew why the latter felt that there could be a chain of bankruptcies of the most important banks in strategic centers.

The fourth personality who has definitely marked the latest stage of capitalist economic development thinking is Milton Friedman. He is the father of the strict supply-side economics applied by many countries throughout the world and which the International Monetary Fund advocates so strongly: the last recourse against the inflationary phenomenon that surged with extraordinary strength after Keynes.

I am here speaking from no other place than Venezuela, Bolívar's glorious homeland

At present, we can find anything: a number of countries immersed in a depression, others in inflation, recipes and measures that destabilize governments. The world has already realized that the International Monetary Fund will economically ruin and politically destabilize the countries it assists or tries to assist. Now more than ever we can rightly say that the assistance of the International Monetary Fund is like the Devil's kiss.

Allow me to point out some facts which I would like to draw to your attention and which respond to the question I asked myself when I said: 'What is the legacy of capitalism and neo-liberal globalization?' After 300 years of capitalism, the world now has 800 million hungry people. Now, at this very moment, there are 1 billion illiterates, 4 billion poor, 250 million children who work regularly and 130 million people that have no access to education. There are 100 million homeless and 11 million children under five years of age dying every year of malnutrition, poverty and preventable or curable diseases.

There is a growing gap between the poor and the rich, within countries and between countries; a callous and almost irreversible destruction of nature; an accelerated squandering and depletion of important non-renewable resources; pollution of the air and underground waters, rivers and oceans; climatic changes with unpredictable but already perceptible consequences. During the past century, more than 1 billion hectares of virgin forests were devastated and a similar area has become either deserts or wastelands.

Thirty years ago hardly anyone discussed these issues; now it is crucial for our species. I do not wish to give any more figures. I believe that these data serve to qualify a system which claims to be perfect, to grant a rating of 100 points, 90, 80, 50, 25, or perhaps less than 25. All this is very easy to demonstrate and its disastrous results may be conceptualized as self-evident truths.

In face of all this, perhaps many are wondering, 'What is to be done?' Well, the Europeans have invented their own recipe. They are uniting. They spoke about a single currency that has already been approved and is now in the process of implementation. The good wishes of the United States, according to spokespersons of that country, have not been lacking, good wishes which are as great as they are hypocritical because everyone knows that what they really want is for the euro to fail. They say, 'What a wonderful thing, this euro is very good, it is an excellent idea'. This is the case of a rich, developed Europe with an annual GDP per capita of 20,000 US dollars in some countries and of 25,000 to 30,000 US dollars in others. Compare these countries with others in our world with 500, 600 or 1000 US dollars.

And what shall we do? This is a question that we must all ask ourselves within this context, at a moment when they are trying to swallow our countries. And you can rest assured that this is what they would like to do. We should not expect another miracle like that when the prophet was delivered from the gut of a whale because if that whale swallowed us, we are really going to be fully digested at full speed.

Yes, this is our hemisphere and I am here speaking from no other place than Venezuela, Bolívar's glorious homeland, where he dreamed, where he conceived the unity of our nations and worked for its attainment at a time when it took three months to travel from Caracas to Lima on horseback and when there were no cellular phones, nor airplanes, nor highways, nor computers, nor anything of the sort. And yet, he realized and foresaw the danger that those few, recently independent colonies, far up North, could pose. He was prophetic when he said, 'The United States seem destined by providence to plague the Americas with misery in the name of liberty'. He launched the idea of our people's unity and struggled for it until his death. If it was a dream then, today it is a vital necessity.

How can solutions be worked out? They are difficult, very difficult. As I said, the Europeans have set a target and are immersed in a tight competition with our neighbour of the North; this is obvious, a strong and growing competition. The United States does not want anyone to interfere with its interests in what it considers to be its hemisphere. It wants everything absolutely for itself. On the other hand, China in the Far East, is a huge nation and Japan is a powerful, industrial country.

I believe that globalization is an irreversible process and that the problem is not globalization *per se*, but rather the type of globalization. This is why it seems to me that for this difficult and tough undertaking, for which the peoples do not have much time, the Latin Americans are the ones who should hurry the most and struggle for unity, agreements and regional integration not only within Latin America but also between Latin America and the Caribbean. There we have our English speaking sister nations of the Caribbean, the CARICOM members, who after barely a few years of independence have acted with impressive dignity.

I say this based on their behaviour towards Cuba. When everybody in Latin America, except for Mexico, severed all ties with our country in response to American pressures, the Caribbean nations, together with Torrijos, were the first to break through. They have struggled to break Cuba's isolation until the present when Cuba maintains relations with the immense majority of the Latin American and Caribbean countries. We know them and we appreciate them. They cannot be left to their own fate, they cannot be left in the hands of the WTO and its agreements. They cannot be left at the mercy of the US banana transnational enterprises, which try to take away the small preferences that they so badly need. You cannot mend the world by levelling everything to the ground; that is the way the Yankees do it, by razing everything.

Several of these countries live from their plantations and produce only 1 per cent of the banana marketed, 2 per cent at the most, which is meaningless. The United States government, to protect a US transnational that owns three plantations in Central America, filed an appeal with the WTO and won. Now the Caribbean nations are very worried because similar procedures may be applied to take these preferences away and because measures are being adopted to liquidate the Lome Convention, by virtue of which they enjoy some considerations as former colonies and countries in dire need of resources for development. It is unfair to take these considerations away from them.

It is not fair to treat all nations equally, as there are marked differences in their levels of development that cannot be ignored. It is not right to use the same recipe for all. It is not right to impose a single formula. Formulas for controlling and developing economic relations are of no avail if they will only benefit the wealthy and the powerful. Bot the IMF and the WTO want everything *tabula rasa*.

The OECD, the exclusive club of the wealthy, was rather secretly preparing a supranational multilateral investment agreement to establish the laws that would govern foreign investment. Something like a worldwide Helms–Burton Law, and all that rather very quietly. They had almost everything ready and then a non-governmental organization got hold of a copy of the draft. The copy was disseminated through internet creating a scandal in France, which rejected such a draft agreement. Apparently they had not paid much attention to what was brewing at the OECD. Later, I think the Australians did the same, consequently the draft was abandoned which had been so secretly worked out.

This is how many important and decisive international treaties are produced. Then, they put the draft on the table so that those who want to sign it may do so and those who do not, well, everyone knows what happens to those who do not want to sign. Not a single word was discussed with the countries that were to apply such unavoidable standards. This is how they treat us. This is how they handle the most vital interests of our peoples.

They will continue. We must be very vigilant and alert with these institutions. We must say that they were laying a big trap for us. So far, we have managed to sidestep it but they will continue with their scheming to make our living conditions even worse. It was not only a matter of competing with everyone and with the whole world making desperate concessions in every field. The Agreement on Multilateral Investments was intended to facilitate their investments in the conditions they deem fit, respecting the environment if they wish, or poisoning the rivers in every country if they feel like it, destroying nature without anyone being able to demand anything from them. But Third World countries are a majority in the WTO and, if we can stop them from deceiving and dividing us, we can fight for our interests. Cuba could not be excluded from the WTO because it belonged to it since its foundation.

But they do not want China in, at least they are putting up great resistance. China is making great efforts to enter the WTO because a 1000 per cent tariff can be applied to countries not belonging to this institution and their exports can be completely blocked. The richest countries are setting the rules and requirements that better suit them.

What is it that suits them? What is it they are after? They want to see the day when there will be no tariffs, when their investments will not be charged by the tax authorities in any country. They obtain years of tax exemption as a concession from underdeveloped countries thirsty for investments where they get the lion's share and the right to do as they please with their investments in our countries with no restriction whatsoever. They also impose the free circulation of capital and goods throughout the world. Of course, the exception is that commodity bearing the name of Third World people who are the modern slave, the cheap manpower so abundant in our planet, flooding the free-trade zones in their own land or sweeping streets, harvesting vegetables and doing the hardest and worst paid jobs when legally or illegally admitted into the former metropolis or into consumer societies.

This is the type of global capitalism they want to impose. Our countries full of free-trade zones would have no other income but the meagre salary of those fortunate enough to get a job, while a bunch of billionaires accumulate fortunes, which no one knows how big they will get.

what year 2000 are we going to celebrate and what kind of a new century will we live in?

The fact that an American citizen, no matter how great his talent and expertise in technology and business matters, owns a 64 billion dollar fortune, which is the annual income of more than 150 million human beings in the poorest countries, is something awesomely unequal and unfair. That this capital has been accumulated over a few years, because the stocks value of the large American enterprises doubles every three or four years through stock exchange transactions inflating the value of assets *ad infinitum*, shows a reality that cannot be considered rational, sustainable or endurable, someone is paying for all that: the world and the astronomic figures of poor, hungry, ill, illiterate and exploited people populating the earth.

What year 2000 are we going to celebrate and what kind of a new century will we live in? Besides, this century does not end on December 31st. People are self-deceived, because the last year in this century is actually the year 2000 and not 1999. However, there will be celebrations and I believe that some will be very happy to celebrate, in a special way, on December 31, 1999, and on December 31, 2000, and those who sell nougat, beverages, Christmas presents, Santa Clauses and all that will do great business with two end-of-the-century days instead of one. France will sell more champagne than ever.

It's all right with me. I spent this last Christmas Eve writing a speech. It is better that way because you do not fall in the temptation of broaching additional topics and issues and you strictly follow what you have promised yourself. That was what I was doing at midnight, this last Christmas Eve but I was happy. It was the eve of the fortieth anniversary of a revolution they were not able to overcome. I was really happy, I cannot pretend otherwise.

The world will reach that 21st century with people living under New York bridges, wrapped in papers, while others amass enormous fortunes. There are many tycoons in that country but the number of those living under bridges, at the entrance of buildings or in slums is incomparably higher. In the United States millions live in critical poverty, something in which the fanatic advocates of the economic order imposed upon humanity cannot take pride.

A few days ago I was talking with an American delegation visiting Cuba, actually well informed, friendly and outstanding religious people and scientists, and they told me that they were engaged in building a pediatric hospital in the Bronx. I asked them: 'Is not there a pediatric hospital in the Bronx?' And they answered: 'No.' 'And how many children are there in the Bronx?' I asked. And they said: 'Four hundred thousand children.' So there are 400,000 children in a city such as New York, many of them of Puerto Rican descent, of Hispanic descent in general, and black, who do not have a pediatric hospital.

But they also said that, 'There are 11 million American children who do not have medical insurance.' They are mostly black, mixed, natives or the children of Hispanic immigrants. Do not think discrimination in that society is based only on the color of the skin, no, it is not. Whether they have blond or dark hair, they are at times treated with contempt simply because they are Latin American. There was a time when I visited that country, then I sat in cafeterias or lived in those motels at the side of the road and more than once I felt their contempt; they almost felt furious to have a Hispanic around. It impressed me as a society full of hatred.

The 11 million children without medical insurance belong, most of them to those minorities living in the United States. They have the highest infant mortality rate. I asked them what was the infant mortality rate in the Bronx and they said they thought it was about 20 or 21 per 1000 live births in the first year of life. There are worse places – in Washington itself it is quite high – and in areas where Hispanic immigrants mostly live it is 30 or 30 odds. It is not the same everywhere.

Their infant mortality is higher than that of Cuba. The blockaded country, the country targeted for their war and from which they stole 3,000 physicians, today has an infant mortality of 7.1 per every 1000 live births. Our rates are better and they are very similar throughout the country. It is 6 in some provinces, not precisely in the capital; it may be 8 in others, but it is within that rank, two or three percentage points of difference with the national average because medical care reaches all social sectors and regions.

Even after the beginning of the special period, in these eight terrible years, we were able to reduce infant mortality to 7.1, from 10 in 1998. It was an almost 30 per cent reduction and that even when we entered a very difficult stage after the demise of the socialist camp and especially the Soviet Union, with which we had most of our trade. Also the US economic war against Cuba grew more sever. In 1993, for example, despite all our efforts, the per capita daily calories intake had declined to 1863 from 3000 and to approximately 46 g of animal or plant protein from 75 g. Oh, but among other essentials, a very inexpensive, subsidized litre of milk was guaranteed to children under 7 years of age.

We have managed to help the most vulnerable groups. If there is a severe drought or any other natural disaster we try to find resources wherever we can to protect everyone, but specially the children and the elderly.

The establishment of new, very important scientific centers has been one of the advances of the Revolution during the special period. Our country produces 90 per cent of its medications, even though some raw materials must be imported from very distant places. We have shortages of medications, that is true, but everything possible has been done to always have the most essential ones in stock, to have a central reserve, in case some may be missing one day, and we are trying to have more reserves. These actions had to be taken because we must anticipate in order to be in capacity to protect those in greatest need. Of course, it is also possible to receive medications sent by relatives abroad; we facilitate it as much as possible, we do not charge anything at all, no tariff is paid for that, but we do all we can for the state to offer these resources to all our population.

Despite the said decline in food consumption, we have been able to reduce infant mortality by 30 per cent, as I said before. We have also maintained and even raised life expectancy. On the other hand, not a single school was closed; not a single teacher lost his job, on the contrary, teacher-training colleges and institutions are open for all those who wish to enroll.

I must clarify that we have not been able to do the same in all professions. In medicine, we have already had to set certain limits, looking for higher qualifications, for a higher quality in those entering the profession because we graduated many physicians in our struggle against our neighbour and we let them migrate if they wanted to. In that battle we established 21 medical colleges.

Right now we are offering 1,000 scholarships to Central American students to be trained as physicians in our country and an additional 500 each year for ten years; we are establishing a Latin American medical college. With the cuts we have made in expenses, even in defense expenses despite the dangers we face, we will be able to locate the medical college in the former facilities of an excellent school for civil and military navy captains and technicians whose school has been moved to another facility. The medical college will be ready in March and the first Central American students will arrive for a six month premedical catch-course to refresh their knowledge and prevent later dropouts. In September more than a thousand Central American students will be studying their first year of medicine in Cuba. I do not know if it is necessary to add that their studies will be absolutely free of charge.

Perhaps I should say – and do not take it as an advertisement for Cuba but as something having to do with the ideas about what can be done with very little – that we offered 2,000 physicians to the Central American countries hit by hurricane Mitch and we have said that, if a developed country or some developed countries – and some have already answered – supply the medications, our medical personnel is ready to save in Central America every year – I repeat, every year! – as many lives as were lost in the hurricane, supposing the hurricane caused no less that 30,000 casualties, as reported. 25,000 of those lives to be saved would be children's.

According to estimates, medications to save a child often cost only a few cents. What cannot be bought at any price is a trained physician ready to work in the mountains, in the remotest places, in swampy areas, full of insects, snakes, mosquitoes and some diseases that do not exist in our country. And none of them hesitate. The immense majority of our physicians have volunteered for that task. They are ready for it and 400 of them are now working in Central America; 250 physicians are already working in Haiti, a country that received the same offer after it was hit by hurricane George.

The percentage of lives that can be saved in Haiti is higher because infant mortality there is 130 or 132. It means that by reducing it to 35 – and in our country we know very well how to do it – 100 children a year for every 1000 live births would be saved. That is why the potential is larger. Its population is 7.5 million, and the birth rate is very high, thus, physicians there may save more lives. In Central America the average rate in the countries hit by the hurricane is about 50 or 60, almost half of the lives that can be potentially saved.

I warn you that these are conservative estimates. There is a margin over and above the figures mentioned. On the other hand, we do not want our physicians working in the cities because we do not want any local physician to be affected in any way by the presence of the Cuban physicians. Cuban physicians offer their services in the places where there are no physicians and where other physicians would not go. On the contrary, we want to have the best relations with local physicians, we want to cooperate with them, whether they are in private practice or not. If they are interested in a case, it is all right with us.

We have said that cooperation with local physicians is necessary and also cooperation with other sectors. Our physicians are not going there to preach political ideas; they are going to accomplish a humane mission. That is their task. There should also be cooperation with priests and pastors, since many of these have been carrying out their work in isolated places. Some of our first physicians to arrive lived in parish facilities.

So they are working in coordination and we are very pleased by it. They are working in intricate places, where there are indigenous people who speak their own language, people with great dignity, and peasants who live in small villages. That facilitates the physicians' work because in Cuba peasants live far from each other in the mountains so they must walk long distances to visit the patients regularly while in a village they can visit more than once a day.

A programme is being implemented there that says much about what can be done with a minimum of material resources. What is most important and those gentlemen, the managers of the financial institutions I have mentioned do not know it, is that there is a capital worth much more than all their millions: the human capital.

the US administration is saying that every American should buy a Cuban well, let us raise the price then

Perhaps, one day I meet one of those assistants to Bill Gates, who is a computing champion, then I will ask him a question: can you tell me how many Americans have served abroad since the Peace Corps was created? Just to know if they are more than the number of Cubans who have done likewise thanks to the generous and cooperative spirit to that very slandered and ignored island and people, against which a war that was not waged against apartheid fascists is being waged. I am speaking about an economic war. I know many decent, altruistic Americans. I know many, and it is a very high merit that so many altruistic people live in a place whose system only sows selfishness and the venom of individualism. I respect these Americans. I have met some that have served with the Peace Corps but I am sure that they have not been able to mobilize, since their creation, the number Cuba has mobilized.

Once, when Nicaragua requested 1,000 teachers – later they asked for some more – we invited volunteers and 30,000 offered. Then, when the bandits organized and supplied by the United States who waged that dirty war against the Sandinistas murdered some of our teachers who were not in the cities, but in the most isolated places in the countryside, sharing the peasants living conditions – 100,000 volunteered to go. This is what I mean! And I must add that most of them were women because women are the majority in that profession.

That is why I am discussing ideas; that is why I am discussing consciousness. That is why I believe what I am saying, that is why I believe in mankind. Because when so many of our fellow countrymen and women went or were ready to go to those places, consciousness and the idea of solidarity and internationalism proved to be a mass phenomenon.

I will complete my idea. I already said that they took half our physicians and more than half of the professors of the only medical college in Cuba. We accepted the challenge – there is nothing like a challenge – and today Cuba has 64,000 physicians, one for every 176 people – twice the number of physicians per capita in the most industrialized of all the countries in the First World. And what I did not say is that since the beginning of the special period we have incorporated 25,000 new physicians in health institutions and communities throughout the country in towns, country, plains and mountains. This is really human capital!

It is much easier to conquer a person than to buy him. Fortunately, it is much easier, because with its so-called easing of the blockade – actually intended to deceive the world – what the US administration is practically saying is that every American should buy a Cuban. I say: well, let us raise the price then, because there are 27 Americans for every Cuban. After all it has done against our country, after intensifying its economic war under the pressure of the extreme right, this administration had the ultimate idea: to buy us one by one. Not ministers, administrative cadre or political leaders but common citizens, by granting every American a permission – always with the Administration's prior consent, of course – to send remittances to Cubans even if they are not related.

I say: very well, now we know we are worth something since there are people willing to pay for us, a very rich government trying to buy us out. There are 4 billion poor in the world and they are not willing to pay a dime for any of them. Our quotation in the market has been climbing.

I am telling you this because we are extending out medical care programme to Surinam, which requested over 60 physicians. Even from a region in Canada, an autonomous province, its authorities requested physicians. They say: 'We do not find physicians wanting to serve in the Arctic Circle. They do not want to come.' We immediately told them: 'Yes, but you discuss it with your government. It is up to you.' Of course, conditions would be different, not because we would profit from it but because it is only logical for things to be different in case of an industrialized country. The physicians' services would be reasonably although modestly remunerated, since what moves us are not economic interests, but sincere wishes for international cooperation in the field of health, in which we have enough human resources.

If the Canadian official can overcome all the obstacles to take the physicians there, we will have Cuban doctors from the Amazonian jungle to the Arctic Circle. But we are focused on the Third World. We pay our physicians their modest salaries in our country. It is good, we are all happy about that and our physicians are very happy with this arrangement, their morale is very high and they come from a great internationalist tradition.

We have received requests for cooperation from other places. Thus, the idea emerged of helping Haiti and later Central America. Now we see it is extending through Latin America and the Caribbean. We have no money, but we have human capital.

You should not think I am boasting when I say that they would have to bring together all the physicians in the United States – I do not know how many they are – to try to find 2,000 volunteers ready to go to the swamps, mountains and inhospitable places where our physicians go. It would be worthwhile to see what would happen, even though I know there are also altruistic physicians over there, that is for sure. But to find 2,000 willing to leave the standard of living a consumer society offers and go to a swamp in Mosquito Coast, a place that not even the Spanish conquerors could stand – and that is really saying something – that, perhaps, they may be unable to do. But Cuban physicians are there: that is human capital. If we take one out of every three physicians, we could offer the rest of Latin America the programme we have offered Haiti and Central America, in places where similar conditions exist, where children and adults die for lack of medical care, in places no one else goes to. We have made the offer and it seems it will be accepted and our country will be in a position to respond. Such is the kind of human capital that can be created!

How many lives can be saved? We have suggested and publicly proclaimed the idea of having the countries in our region unite to save a million lives every year, including the lives of hundreds of thousands children. The cost of saving a million lives can be accurately estimated and saving the lives of children is the least costly, because older people need more laboratory tests and radiography, more medications and all that while children survive almost by themselves after the first year of life. At times a vaccine worth a few cents saves a life. Polio is a case in point.

We believe that a million lives can be saved every year with a small part of the money wasted in extravagant expenditures and there are physicians ready for the task. There may be more than enough medications in Europe but they will not save a million lives without the 15,000 to 20,000 physicians required to undertake a programme such as this.

I am telling you about this so you know what Cuba is today, why Cuba is like that and what the prevailing standards are in Cuba, a country so miserably slandered in matters of human rights. A country where in forty years of Revolution there has never been a missing person, where there has never been a tortured person, where there are no death squads and no political assassinations and nothing like that has ever happened. A country where there are no elderly people abandoned, no children living in the streets, without schools or teachers, no people left to their own lot.

We very well know what has happened in some of the places where our neighbours from the North have been, such as those who organized in 1954 the ousting of the government in one of the most important countries in the Central American region. They brought in their advisers with their handbooks on torture, repression and death. For many years there were no prisoners, this category did not exist, only dead and missing persons. A hundred thousand missing persons in just one country! And fifty thousand killed. We could add what happened in many other countries with tortures, murders, missing persons, repeated US military interventions under any pretext or no pretext at all.

They do not remember that, they do not speak about that, they have lost their memory. In the light of the terrible experience undergone by the peoples of our America, we challenge them. We will demonstrate with actual facts, with realities, who has a humane sense of life, who has true humanitarian feelings and who is capable of doing something for mankind that is not lies, slogans, misinformation, hypocrisy, deception and all they have been doing in our region throughout this century.

I know you do not need me to clarify all this to you but since I broached the subject I feel it is my duty to say so. It is very often that one meets misinformed persons who believe at least some of the tons of lies and slanders that have been cast against our country, in an attempt to hit us, to weaken us, to isolate us, to divide us. They have not been able to divide us and they won't be able to!

it is easier to control the seven dwarfs than to control a boxer

I have said all these things to you in the greatest intimacy. I could not come now and speak to you as I did in 1959 about organizing an expedition to solve a problem in a neighbouring country. We very well know that today no country can solve its problems by itself. That is a reality in this globalized world. We can say here: 'Either we are all saved or we all sink.'

Martí said: 'Humanity is my homeland.' This is one of the most extraordinary things he said. That is how we have to think: Humanity is homeland!

I remember a case in Cuban history of a Spanish officer who during the Ten Years War – the first war for the independence of Cuba – when the Spanish government executed eight innocent medical students accused of desecrating the tomb of a rightist Spanish extremist, broke his sword in an imperishable gesture of indignation and protest and exclaimed: 'Humanity comes before one's motherland.' Of course, some parts of mankind are closer from home. When we think of mankind, the first thing that comes to our mind is our Latin American and Caribbean brothers and sisters, whom we never forget. Then comes the rest of that humanity on our planet. We will have to learn that concept, those principles contained in Martí's words – not only learn them, but feel them and practice them.

It is the Latin American countries' duty to unity without losing a single minute; the Africans are trying to do it. In Southeast Asia they have the ASEAN and are looking for other forms of economic integration. Europe is doing it at a swift pace. That is, there will be sub-regional and regional alliances in various parts of the world.

Bolívar dreamed of an extended regional federation from Mexico to Argentina. As you well know, the gentlemen from the North sabotaged the Amphictyonic Congress. They opposed Bolívar's idea of sending an expedition commanded by Sucre to liberate the island of Cuba and remove all risks of threat or counterattack by the fearful and tenacious Spanish metropolis; so we were not forgotten in Venezuelan history. Now that we are free from the domination of a much stronger power, our most sacred duty is to defend our freedom for the very interest and security of our brothers and sisters in this hemisphere.

Obviously, we must work out various forms of cooperation and integration, step by step, but with swift steps if we want to survive as a regional entity with the same culture, the same language and so many things in common. This is something that Europe does not have. I do not know how an Italian understands an Austrian or a Finn, how a German speaks with a Belgian or a Portuguese. But they have been able to create the European Union and they quickly advance towards a larger economic integration and a total monetary union. Why can we not be capable of at least considering this type of formulae? Why do we not encourage all the unitary and integrationist trends in every country sharing our language, our culture, our beliefs and the mixed blood running through the immense majority of us? And, where there is no mixed blood in our veins, there should be mixed blood in our souls.

Who were those who fought in the Ayacucho battle? Men from the lowlands and from Caracas; Venezuelans from the West and the East, Colombians, Peruvians and Ecuadorians who were together and that is how they could do what they did. The unforgettable cooperation of Argentineans and Chileans was also present. Our greatest sin is that we lost, after almost 200 years.

Eleven years from now we will celebrate the 200th anniversary of the proclamation of the Venezuelan Independence and later, in succession, that of the other countries. Almost two hundred years! What have we done in those 200 years, divided, fragmented, Balkanized, submitted as we have been? It is easier to control the seven dwarfs than to control a boxer, even if he is a lightweight. They have wanted to keep us as divided neighbouring dwarfs so they can control us.

I was discussing the need for unity not only in South America but in Central America and the Caribbean as well, and this is the moment to state it given what is happening in Venezuela. They have tried to divide us. The great power in the North wants FTAA and nothing more; a Free

Trade Agreement and fast-track – I believe fast-track means quick, right? A quick step? Yes, I also recommend a fast-track for us, a fast-track to unite. The Latin American answer to the fast-track from the North should be a fast-track from the Center and the South.

Brazil should have our support and encouragement. We very well know that the United States does not like the existence of MERCOSUR, for it is an important embryo of an alliance that may become wider and grow. Some neighbouring countries are not too far away from MERCOSUR. We see it as a sub-regional alliance, as a step toward a regional alliance, first of South America and then another step, as quick as possible to embrace the Caribbean and Central America.

We are considering the need to advance in the contacts, the concept, the arrangements and the practical steps that may be taken in that direction before we can afford to consider the creation of a common currency. We believe that in that field the most we can do right now is to elaborate ideas and concepts. Meanwhile, we need to avoid, at all cost, the political and economic suicide of replacing our national currencies with the American currency, no matter the difficulties and fluctuations imposed by the present economic order. That would be tantamount to the annexation of Latin America to the United States. We would not be considered independent nations any more and we would be renouncing every possibility of taking part in the structuring of the future world. Under the present circumstances it is absolutely indispensable to unite, to come together and to expand our forces.

The meeting of the Caribbean Basin states will be held in the Dominican Republic in April. Later, almost immediately, there will be a meeting with the European Union in Rio de Janeiro. We have some common interests with the Europeans; they are interested in some of our things and we are interested in some of theirs. Living under the slavery of only one currency, as we are now, is a tragedy and we are happy that with the euro, a rival to the Olympic champion, to the gold medal winner, has come into being.

The strengthening of the United Nations is another necessity that cannot be deferred. The United Nations must be democratized. The General Assembly, where all the member countries are represented, should be granted the highest authority, as well as the functions and role befitting it. The Security Council's dictatorship must end together with the dictatorship the United States exercises within that body.

If the veto power cannot be eliminated because those who have the last word about such a reform are precisely those with the power to veto it, we strongly demand that the privilege be at least shared. The number of permanent members must be suitably increased from the five they are now in compliance with the growth of the UN membership and the great changes that have taken place in fifty years. The Third World, where a great number of countries emerged as independent States after World War II, should have the possibility to share equal prerogatives in that important United Nations body. We have defended the idea of having two representatives for Latin America and the Caribbean basin, two for Africa and two for the underdeveloped regions in Asia, as a minimum. If two are not enough, the figure could be increased to three, in one or more of the above mentioned regions. We constitute the immense majority at the United Nations General Assembly and cannot continue being ignored.

We would not oppose the admission of other industrialized countries but we give absolute priority to the presence of permanent representatives of Latin America and the Caribbean and the other above mentioned regions in the Security Council, with the same prerogatives of its other permanent members. If it is not so, we will have three categories of members: permanent members with veto power, permanent members without veto power and non-permanent members. And there is still more of this madness. Aimed at dividing and thus preserving the privileges of their present status, at the same time it reduces the prerogatives of the potential new permanent members, the United States has come up with the idea of rotating that condition among two or more countries from the various regions; that is, to reduce this vital reform to zero, to nothing, to simple salt and water.

There is another way to regulate the irritating veto prerogative with an increase in the number of members needed to apply it, that is, the General Assembly may be given the possibility of taking part in the main decisions. Would not this be more democratic and fair?

A battle must be waged there. All the Third World countries should unite. We say that to Africans when we meet with them, also to Asians, to the Caribbeans, to everyone in every international agency: the United Nations, the Non-Aligned Countries Movement, the Lome meetings, the Group of 77, everywhere. We are a large number of countries sharing common interests, wishing to advance and develop; we are the overwhelming majority in almost all international institutions and you may rest assured that we are advancing in building an awareness about the fate reserved to us. We must work, persuade, fight and persevere. We must never be discouraged.

Those in the North are constantly scheming to divide us. I am going to give you four examples having to do with Latin America.

They do not like MERCOSUR that has already achieved some measure of economic success even though it is but an embryo of the great regional integration we hope for, and they do not want at all. What is it they devise? Well, many things. First, they organize those hemispheric meetings leaving out Cuba, a reaction to the first Ibero–American Summit in Guadalajara.

They devise the idea of having only one Latin American permanent member in the Security Council, to have several important members of our region confronting each other. They immediately add the advisability of rotating the position among Brazil, Argentina and Mexico, of course, with no veto power. Then, they create the special category of strategic ally for Argentina. That plants distrust and restlessness among important fraternal neighbours that should closely unite and cooperate, particularly now when MERCOSUR is advancing.

They invent the Machiavellian decision of releasing the sale of sophisticated arms to countries in the region, which may unleash a costly, destructive and fissiparous arms race among them. Why arms when there is neither a Cold War nor the ghost of the Soviet Union or any other foreign threat to security but that coming from the United States itself? Can these arms contribute to the unity, cooperation, integration, progress and peace among us? What do we need to open up our eyes and finally understand the geo-strategic purposes of this policy?

They have not been able to continue leaving our small country out everywhere. We already take part in the Ibero–American Summits. We are members of the Association of Caribbean States. We belong to the Latin American Economic System and have been included in the Latin American Integration Association. We maintain excellent relations with the Caribbean Community (CARICOM). We will be present in the important Summit of the European Union, Latin America and the Caribbean to be held in Rio de Janeiro. We have been admitted as observers

among the countries in the Lome Convention. We are active members of
the Group of 77 and hold an outstanding place as founding members of
the Non-Aligned Movement. We belong to the WTO and are very present
at the United Nations, which is a great forum and an institution that, once
democratized, may become a basic pillar for a fair and humane
globalization.

What are we doing there? Talking, explaining, submitting
problems that we know touch a large part of mankind very dearly because
we are free to do it. There are brotherly countries in Africa, Asia, Latin
America and other places that would like to submit many things with much
energy but do not have the same possibilities Cuba has. Being already
excluded from all international financial institutions, blockaded and
submitted to an economic warfare, invulnerable to any retaliation of that
type, strengthened by forty years of hard long struggle which gives us an
absolute liberty to do anything, Cuba can speak up. They may be in crucial
need of a credit from the World Bank or from the Inter-American Bank
or from another regional bank, or of some negotiation with the
International Monetary Fund, or of an export credit, which is one of the
many mechanisms used by the United States to limit their possibilities of
action. That is why quite often Cuba has taken upon itself such a task.

In spite of everything, there are people in our impoverished world
who are so courageous that, for example, at the United Nations, the Cuban
motion against the blockade received the support of 157 votes against 2.
We had spent seven years in this exercise. The first time there were some
55 votes in favour and four or five against and all the rest, abstentions or
absences. Who could want to be at odds with the Yankees? Because voting
there is by show of hands.

But people lose fear, and fear was gradually lost; dignity may grow
and it does. The following year, there were more than sixty, then more
than seventy, then over a hundred. Now, after we have the support of
almost 160 countries and only two are against, it can hardly grow anymore.
In the end, there will be no country supporting this inhuman, cruel and
unlimited action except the United States, unless a day comes when the
United States votes for us and supports the Cuban motion.

We are making progress, gaining ground. The people know,
intuitively or instinctively, that we are very often slandered. The people

have a great instinct! Besides, the people know them because they are everywhere doing all sorts of things, abusing people and sowing selfishness and hatred. People know them. Contempt is difficult to hide and the Third World countries suffer under such arrogance and contempt.

The various US administrations with their blockade, their constant harassment and their exclusions have given us the possibility of fighting them in full and of being even joyful to be excluded in exchange for the freedom to speak without compromise in any forum of the world where there are so many fair causes to defend.

For the reasons I have already explained, we may have some sympathies with other countries. As for them, who are the main stronghold of reaction and injustice in our times, we can say the truth and always the truth, with and without relations, with and without a blockade. They should entertain no illusions that, if some day they lift the blockade, Cuba will stop speaking as frankly and honestly as it has done for forty years! It is a historic duty.

Bolívar, the Liberator, greatest among the great men in history

I will finish in a minute, if you allow me. Remember I am a visitor here and I am here before you, before the university students. I am in this country that I sincerely admire and deeply love. I am not flattering you. I was always very fond of history. The first thing I studied was precisely history because when I began the first grade they immediately handed me a book on sacred history where I learned some things I still remember. Of course, I learned about the history of the Ark, the Exodus, the battles and the crossing of the Red Sea. At times, when I speak with some rabbi friends and I ask them: 'Tell me the truth, where did you turn?' – in jest, because I really respect religions and I have considered it an elementary duty to respect the beliefs of every individual.

At times I discuss even theological issues about the world, the universe. When the Pope visited Cuba, I had the satisfaction and the opportunity of meeting some very intelligent theologians whom I bombed with every type of questions. I did not dare ask any of them about dogma or matters of faith but I did ask other types of questions about space, universe, the theories about its origin, the possibilities of there being life on other planets and things that can be very seriously dealt with. With seriousness and respect you can talk about any topic, and based on that respect ask questions and at times even make jokes.

Well, here I am and I was going to tell you that I should say something about Venezuela, right? If you allow me to. You are going to say: 'He came to Venezuela and did not say anything about us.' Let me warn you that this is not an easy task, for the reasons I have already explained.

I began telling you that it is a country I love dearly. This is when I began to tell you about my love for history, for universal history, for the history of revolutions and wars, for the history of Cuba, the history of Latin America, and especially for that of Venezuela. That is why I identified myself so much with Bolívar's life and ideas.

Fate would have it that Venezuela should be the country to fight the most for the independence of this hemisphere. It began here and you had a legendary precursor like Miranda, who even led a French army in campaign waging famous battles which, at a point in time, during the French Revolution, prevented an invasion of French territory. He had also fought in the United States for that country's independence. I have a wide collection of books about Miranda's great life, although I have not been able to read them all. The Venezuelans, therefore, had Miranda, the forefather of Latin America's independence, and later Bolívar, the Liberator, who was always for me the greatest among the great men in history. [*Shouts from the audience: 'Fidel too!'*]

Please, put me in the forty-thousandth place. I always remember one of Martí's phrases deeply engraved in my mind: 'All the glory in the world can fit into a kernel of corn.' Many great people in history were concerned about glory and that is no reason to criticize them. Perhaps it was the concept of time, the sense of history, the future, the importance and survival of events in their lives what they took for glory. This is natural and understandable. Bolívar liked to speak about glory and he spoke very strongly about glory. He cannot be criticized; a great aura of glory will forever be attached to his name.

Martí's concept, which I entirely share, associates glory to personal vanity and self-exaltation. The role of the individual in important historic events has been very much debated and even admitted. What I especially like about Martí's phrase is the idea of man's insignificance as compared to the enormous significance and transcendence of humanity and the immeasurable reach of universe, the reality that we are really like a small speck of dust floating in space. However, that reality does not diminish man's greatness a single bit. On the contrary, it is enhanced when, like in Bolívar's case, he carried in his mind a whole universe full of just ideas and noble sentiments. That is why I admire Bolívar so much. That is why I consider his work so immense. He does not belong to the stock of men who conquered territories and nations, or founded empires that gave fame to others; he created nations, freed territories and tore empires. He was also a brilliant soldier, a distinguished thinker and prophet.

Today, we are trying to do what he wanted to do and remains to be done. We are trying to unite our peoples so that tomorrow, following the same train of unitary thought, the only one which corresponds with our specie and our age, human beings will be able to know and live in a united, brotherly, just and free world. That is what he wanted to do with the white, black, native and mixed peoples of our America.

Here we are in this land for which we feel special admiration, respect and love. When I came 40 years ago, I expressed it with deep gratitude because nowhere else was I better received, with so much affection and enthusiasm. The only thing I could be ashamed of is that I was actually in kindergarten when that first meeting in this prestigious university was held.

Having said this, I will now express, as briefly as possible, the reflection I wanted to make about Venezuela. I am sure not all of your will agree with it. The idea is to make an honest, calm and objective analysis.

Figures and data this visitor has tried to analyse lead him to the conclusion that in this new dawn the people of Venezuela will have to face courageously and intelligently serious difficulties arising from the current economic situation.

Commodity exports according to Central Bank report: in 1997, 23.4 billion US dollars (services, which have almost balanced expenditures and income, are not included here); in 1998, 17.32 billion. In other words, the value of exports dropped by 6.080 million US dollars in only one year.

Oil (the main export item) prices: in 1996, around 20 US dollars per barrel; in 1997, 16.50 US dollars; in 1998, around 9 US dollars.

The basic minerals – iron, aluminum, gold and by-products like steel – have all, to a greater or lesser degree, significantly dropped in price.

Both items make up 77 per cent of exports – I mean, oil and minerals.

Favourable balance of trade: in 1996, 13.6 billion US dollars; in 1998, 3.4 billion – difference: 10.2 billion in just two years.

Balance of payment: in 1996, 7 billion, favourable to Venezuela; in 1998, 3.42 billion, unfavourable to the country; difference: more than 10 billion.

International reserves available: in 1997, 17.818 million US dollars; in 1998, 14.385 million; net losses: approximately 3.5 billion in one year.

Foreign debt: in 1998, 31.6 billion, not including the private short-term financial debt. Almost 40 per cent of the country's budget is spent servicing the foreign debt.

Social situation according to different national and international sources literally ratified yesterday by president Chavez:

Unemployment, he said: official figures report 11 to 12 per cent; other figures indicate 20 per cent.

Underemployment (which supposedly includes unemployment) – the parenthetical expression is mine – is around 50 per cent.

Almost a million children in a state of survival – his own terms.

Infant mortality is almost 28 per 1000 live births. 15 per cent of those deaths are due to malnutrition.

Deficit in housing: 1.5 million.

Only one in 5 children completes grammar school; 45 per cent of adolescents do not attend secondary school.

If you allow me, I will give you an example: 95 per cent of children of that age are in secondary school in Cuba. That is almost as high as you can go. I say this because 45 per cent children out of school is really an impressive figure.

To these data given by the President in his tight synthesis, we could add others taken from various, reliable sources.

More than a million children are in the labour market; over 2.3 million, who are out of the school system, have no trade whatsoever.

In the last ten years, more than a million Venezuelans who belonged to the middle class 'c' category – as you can see, there are also categories within the middle class – fell to the category of poor and destitute, amounting today to 77 per cent of the population. This is due to a drop in incomes, unemployment and the effects of inflation. This means that categories 'c', 'd' and 'e' include today from the poor to the destitute.

This was occurring, as President Chavez said with meaningful and bitter words, in Bolívar's original homeland, the country in the Americas which is the richest in natural resources, has almost one million square kilometers and a population of no more than 22 million.

I am trying to meditate with you here.

I must say, first and foremost, that I am a friend of Chavez's, but no one asked me to address any special issue. No official in his team, no Venezuelan politician or friend knew absolutely anything about what I was going to talk about this afternoon here, in such an important and strategic place as the Central University of Venezuela. I am offering this reflections under my total and absolute responsibility in the hope that they can be useful.

What are we worried about? I seem to perceive at this moment an exceptional situation in the history of Venezuela. I have witnessed two unique moments: first that moment in January 1959, and forty years later, I have seen the extraordinary volatility of the people on February 2, 1999. I have seen a people reborn. A people such as I saw in Plaza del Silencio [Silence Square] where I was a bit more silent than I have been here . . . I even had to reply to an excellent citizen of Caracas, because in fulfilling my elementary duty as a visitor, I mentioned a few personalities that were in the government, beginning with Admiral Larrazábal, and when I mentioned another important political personality of the time, there was noise, protests, which, in turn, made me protest. I complained because that really embarrassed me. I think I even blushed. I told them: 'I am not mentioning names here for you to boo.' I expressed my complaint to the multitude gathered there at Plaza del Silencio. Those were unquestionably revolutionary masses.

It was once again very impressive to see the people in such extraordinary high spirits although under different circumstances. Back then, hopes had been left behind. I do not want to explain why; I leave that to the historians. This time hope lies ahead. I see in these hopes a true rebirth of Venezuela, or at least an exceptionally great opportunity for Venezuela. I see it coming not only in the interest of the Venezuelans, I also see it in the interest of Latin Americans. I see it as something in the interest of other peoples in the world, as it advances – because there is no other choice – towards a universal globalization.

There is no way of escaping it, and there is no alternative. So I am not trying to flatter you with my words. I rather remind you of your duty, the duty of the nation, of the people, of all those who were born after that visit, of the youngest, of the more mature, who really have a great responsibility ahead of you. I think opportunities have often been lost, but you would not be forgiven if you lose this one.

the pleasure of saying all that I thought, everything, quite defiantly

The person speaking to you here has had the privilege and the opportunity of accumulating some political experience, of having lived through a revolutionary process in a country where, as I have already said, people did not even want to hear about socialism. And when I say people, I mean the vast majority. That same majority supported the Revolution, supported the leaders, supported the Rebel Army but there were ghosts they were afraid of. What Pavlov did with his famous dogs, it is the same thing the United States did with many of us and who knows with how many millions of Latin Americans: create conditioned reflexes in us.

We have had to fight a lot against scarcity and poverty. We have had to learn to do a lot with little. We had good and bad moments, the former especially when we were able to establish trade agreements with the socialist block and the Soviet Union and demanded fairer prices for our export products. Because we observed how the prices of what they exported rose while those of our products, in the course of a five-year trade agreement, remained the same. Then, at the end of the five-year period, we had less purchasing power. We proposed a sliding clause: when the prices of the products that they exported to us rose, the prices of the products that we exported to them also automatically rose. We resorted to diplomacy, to the doctrine and the eloquence that revolutionaries in a country that had to overcome so many obstacles must have.

Actually, the Soviets felt great sympathy for Cuba and great admiration for our Revolution. It was very surprising for them to see that after so many years a tiny country, right next to the United States, would rebel against that mighty superpower. They had never contemplated such possibility and they would have never advised it to anyone. Luckily we never asked anybody for advise, although we had already read almost a whole library of the works of Marx, Engels, Lenin and other theoreticians. We were convinced Marxists and socialists.

With that fever and that blind passion that characterizes young people, and sometimes old people too, I assumed the basic principles that I learned from those books and they helped me understand the society where I lived. Until then it was for me an intricate entanglement for which I could not find any convincing explanation. I must say that the famous *Communist Manifesto*, which Marx and Engels took so long to write – you can tell that its main author worked conscientiously, a phrase he liked to use, and must have revised it more times than Balzac revised each page of any of his novels – impressed me tremendously because for the first time in my life I realized a few truths that I had never seen before.

Before that, I was a sort of utopian communist. I began to draw my own conclusions and ended up being a utopian communist while studying from an enormous book with some 900 mimeographed pages, the first political economy course they taught us in Law School. It was a political economy inspired in the ideas of capitalism but which mentioned and analysed very briefly the different schools and criteria. Later, in the second course, I paid much attention to the subject and meditated on the basis of rational viewpoints, so I ended up being a utopian communist. I call it that because my doctrine had no scientific or historic basis whatsoever. It was based on the good wishes of a student recently graduated from a Jesuits' school. And I am very grateful because they taught me some things that have helped me in life, above all, to have strength, a certain sense of honour and definite ethical principles that these Spanish Jesuits – although very distant from any of the ideas I uphold today – instilled in their pupils.

I came out of that school an athlete, an explorer and a mountain climber. I entered the University of Havana ignorant about politics, without a revolutionary private tutor who would have been so useful to me at that stage of my life.

That is how I came to have my own ideas, which I preserve and maintain with growing loyalty and fervour. Maybe it is because I now have a little more experience and knowledge, and maybe also because I have had the opportunity of meditating about new problems that did not even exist during Marx's time.

For example, the word *environment* was probably never pronounced by anyone in all of Karl Marx's life, except Malthus who said that the population grew in geometric progression and that there would not be enough food for so many people. He thus became a sort of forerunner of today's sociologists, although he maintained ideas concerning the economy and salaries we cannot but disagree with.

So I am wearing the same coat I wore when I came to this university 40 years ago, the same one I wore when I attacked the Moncada garrison, when we disembarked from *Granma*. I would venture to say, despite the many pages of adventure that anyone can find in my revolutionary life, that I always tried to be wise and sensible, although perhaps I have been wiser than sensible.

In our conception and development of the Cuban Revolution, we acted as Martí said when, on the eve of his death in combat, he addressed the great anti-imperialist objective of his struggle: 'It had to be in silence and sort of indirectly since the achievement of certain goals demands concealment, for, if proclaimed for what they really are, obstacles so formidable would rise as to prevent their attainment.'

I was discreet, but not as much as I should have been because I would explain Marx's ideas and the class society to everyone I met. So, in the people's movement whose slogan in its fight against corruption was 'Dignity against Money' which I had joined as soon as I arrived at the university, they were beginning to take me for a communist. Towards the end of my university studies, I was no longer a utopian communist but rather an atypical communist who was acting freely. I based myself in a realistic analysis of our country's situation.

Those were the times of McCarthyism and Cuba's Marxist party, the People's Socialist Party was almost completely isolated. However, within the movement I had joined, which had now become the Cuban People's Party, a large mass, in my opinion, had a class instinct but lacked a class consciousness – peasants, workers, professionals, middle-class people – good, honest, potentially revolutionary people. Its founder and leader, a man of great charisma, had dramatically taken his own life a few months before the 1952 *coup d'état*. The younger ranks of that party later became an important part of our movement.

I was a member of that political organization which, as it usually happened, was already falling into the hands of rich people, and I knew by heart what was going to happen after the then inevitable electoral triumph. But I had come up with some ideas, also on my own – just imagine the things a utopian can think up – about what had to be done in Cuba and how to do it, despite the United States. Those masses had to be led along a revolutionary path. Maybe that was the merit of the tactic we pursued. Of course, we were reading Marx's, Engels's and Lenin's books.

When we attacked the Moncada garrison we left one of Lenin's books behind, and the first thing the propaganda of Batista's regime said during the trial was that it was a conspiracy of corrupt members of the recently overthrown government, bankrolled with their money, and communist too. No one knows how both categories could be reconciled.

In the trial, I assumed my own defense. It was not that I thought myself a good lawyer but I thought that I was the person who could best defend myself at that moment. I put on a gown and took my place with the lawyers. It was a political and not a penal trial. I did not intend to be acquitted but to disseminate ideas. I began to cross-examine all those killers who had murdered dozens upon dozens of our comrades and were there as witnesses; I turned the trial against them. So the next day they took me out of there, they put me away and declared me ill.

That was the last thing they did although they really wanted to do away with me once and for all; but, well, I knew very well why they checked themselves. I knew and I know the psychology of all of those people. It was due to the mood and the situation with the people, the rejection and huge indignation caused by all the murders they had committed. I also had a bit of luck. But the fact is that at the beginning, while they were questioning me, this book of Lenin appears. Someone takes it out and says: 'You people had a book of Lenin.'

We were explaining who we were: Martí followers, that was the truth, that we had nothing to do with that corrupt government that they had ousted from power, that our objectives were such and such. However, we did not say a word about Marxism-Leninism, neither did we have to. We said what we had to say but since the subject of the book came up at the trial, I felt irritated and said, 'Yes, that book by Lenin is ours, we read Lenin's books and other socialist books, and whoever does not read them is an ignorant.' That is what I told the judges and the rest of the people there. That was insufferable. We were not going to say: 'Listen, that little book was planted there by somebody . . .'

Our programme had been presented when I defended myself at the trial, therefore, those who did not know how we thought was because they did not want to know. Perhaps they tried to ignore that speech known as *History Will Absolve Me* with which I defended myself all alone over there. Because, as I have explained, I was expelled, they declared me ill, they tried all the others and sent me to a hospital to try me, in a small ward. They did not exactly hospitalize me, but put me in an isolated prison cell. In the hospital, they turned a small ward into a courtroom with the judges and a few other people crammed into it, most of them from the military. They tried me there, and I had the pleasure of saying there all that I thought, everything, quite defiantly.

I wonder why they were not able to deduce what our political thought was, for it was all there. It contained, you might say, the foundation of a socialist government programme although we were convinced the time was not ripe, that the right time and stages would come. That was when we spoke about the land reform among many other things of a social and economic nature. We said that all the profits obtained by all those gentlemen with so much money – that is, the surplus value but without using such terminology – should be used for the development of the country, and I hinted that it was the government's responsibility to look after the development of the country and that surplus money.

I even spoke about the golden calf. I recalled the Bible once again and singled out 'those who worshipped the golden calf', in a clear reference to those who expected everything from capitalism. Those were elements enough for them to deduce our way of thinking.

Later, I have meditated that it is likely that many of those who could be affected by a true revolution did not believe us at all, because in the 57 years of Yankee neocolonialism, many a progressive or revolutionary programme had been proclaimed. The ruling classes never believed our programme to be possible or permissible by the United States. They did not pay much attention to it. They heeded it and even found it funny. At the end of the day, all the programmes used to be abandoned and people would become corrupt. So they probably said: 'Yes, the illusions of these romantic young men are very pretty, very nice, but, why worry about that?'

They did not like Batista. They admired the frontal fight against his abusive and corrupt regime and they possibly underestimated the thoughts contained in that declaration, which were the basis of what we later did and of what we think today. The difference is that many years of experience have further enriched our knowledge and perceptions about all those problems. So, as I have said, that is the way I have thought since then.

in times of scarcity, real scarcity, you learn quite a lot

We have undergone the tough experience of a long revolutionary period, especially during the last ten years, confronting extremely powerful forces under very difficult circumstances. Well, I will tell you the truth: we achieved what seemed impossible. I would venture to say that near miracles were performed. Of course, the laws were passed exactly as they had been promised always with angry and arrogant opposition from the United States. It had had great influence in our country, so it made itself felt and the process became increasingly radicalized with each blow and aggression we suffered.

Thus began the long struggle we have waged until today. The forces in our country polarized. Fortunately, the vast majority was in favour of the Revolution and a minority, around 10 per cent or less, was against it. So there has always been a great consensus and a great support for all that process until today. One knows what to worry about, because we made a great effort to overcome the prejudices that existed, to convey ideas, to build a consciousness and it was not easy work.

I remember the first time I spoke about racial discrimination. I had to go on television about three times. I was surprised at how deeply rooted, more than we had supposed, had become the prejudices brought to us by our northern neighbours: that certain clubs were for white people only and the rest could not go there, as well as certain beaches. Almost all the beaches, especially in the capital, were exclusively for whites. There were even segregated parks and promenades, where according to the colour of your skin you had to walk in one direction or another. What we did was to open all the beaches for all of the people and from the very first days we prohibited discrimination in all places of recreation, parks and promenades. That humiliating injustice was incompatible with the Revolution.

One day I spoke and I explained these things. There was such reaction, such rumours and so many lies! They said we were going to force white men into marrying black women and white women into marrying black men. Well, just like that other preposterous invention that we were going to deprive families of the parental custody of their children. I once again had to go on television on the subject of discrimination to reply to all those rumours and machinations and explain the matter once again. That phenomenon, which was nothing but an imposed racist culture, a humiliating, cruel prejudice was very hard to eradicate.

In other words, during those years, we devoted a great deal of our time to two things: defending ourselves from expeditions, threats of foreign aggression, dirty war, assassination attempts, sabotages, etc., and building consciousness. There was a moment when there were armed mercenary bands in every province of our country, promoted and supplied by the United States. But we confronted them immediately, we gave them no time. They had not the slightest chance to prosper because our own experience in irregular warfare was very recent and we were practically one of the few revolutionary countries which totally defeated these bands despite the logistic support they received from abroad. We had to devote a lot of our time to that.

One problem I see, one source of concern I have is that many expectations have been raised in Venezuela by the extraordinary results of the elections, and it is logical. What do I mean? I mean the natural, logical tendency of the people to dream, to wish that a great number of accumulated problems be solved in a matter of months. As an honest friend of yours, in my own opinion, I think there are problems here that will not be solved in months, or years.

That is why I read the data. Because we are daily looking at and analysing similar data in our country: the price of nickel or sugar; the yield of a hectare of sugar cane; if there is a drought, if there is not; how much income we are getting; how much we owe; what must be purchased urgently; what the prices of powdered milk, cereals, indispensable medicines, inputs for production and all the other things are and what is to be done.

At a given point in time our sugar production was boosted, almost doubled. There were good prices, we purchased machinery and began to build the infrastructure. Investments in industry and agriculture increased, limited only by Soviet technological resources, which were more advanced in some fields and less advanced in others. They generally consumed too much fuel.

But we bought all the steel we needed that was not covered by our national production. Half a million cubic meters of timber arrived in Cuba from Siberia every year, purchased with sugar, nickel and other products that, thanks to the sliding prices – the agreement we had reached before the oil prices surged – increased their prices as the price of oil increased. And do you know how much we got to consume? Thirteen million tons a year. Not only due to all the transportation services, the mechanization of agriculture and port facilities, the construction of tens of thousands of kilometers of highway, hundreds of big and small dams, mainly for agriculture, houses, dairy farms, all equipped with milking machines, thousands of schools and other social facilities, but also because of the power consumption in industries and homes. The electrification of the country benefited 95 per cent of the population. There were resources but I could add that we were not even able to manage them with maximum efficiency.

Now we do, we have learned. In times of abundance, you do not learn much, but in times of scarcity, real scarcity, you learn quite a lot. But we did all those things that allowed us to achieve these results in the economic, social and other spheres I have talked about.

Our country also holds first place in education, in teachers per capita. Recently, UNESCO issued a very rewarding report. A survey was conducted among 54,000 children in the third and fourth grade of grammar school about their knowledge of mathematics and language, in fourteen Latin American countries, among the most advanced. An average was obtained: some were above the average and others were below but Cuba ranked first by a wide margin, almost twice the average of the rest of Latin America. In all the parameters, such as students' age per grade, retention rate, non-repeating students and other factors which measure the quality of grammar school, we hold, without exception, the place of honour, placing our country, all by itself, in category 1.

There are a large number of new teachers and every passing year they accumulate more knowledge and experience, just like there is a large number of doctors who gather more and more knowledge with each passing year. The same thing happens with professionals in general and several fields in particular. The percentage of the gross income that we invest in science is incomparably higher than that of the most advanced countries in Latin America, with tens of thousands of scientific workers, many of them with postgraduate degrees and constantly raising their knowledge. We have done a lot of things and invested mainly in human capital.

What do I fear? It is this, which I frankly say here and I am willing to say anywhere. You people lived through periods of abundance. [*Shouts from the audience: 'That was very long ago.'*] Okay, long ago. In 1972 the price of oil was 1.90 US dollars a barrel. For example, at the triumph of the Revolution, Cuba could buy the 4 million tons of fuel it consumed with a few hundred thousand tons of sugar, at the normal world sugar price existing then. When the price of fuel suddenly rose we were saved by the already mentioned sliding price. But when the crisis came – after the USSR was lost and our basic market with it, as well as all our agreed prices – we had to cut by half the 13 million tons of oil which was our consumption by then. A large part of what we were exporting we had to invest in fuel, and we learned to save.

I have already talked about baseball players. I would add that in every small village there were baseball players and they would use tractors and wagons to transport the players and fans to the games. And there were even some tractor drivers who used them to go visit their sweethearts. We had gone from 5,000 tractors to 80,000.

The people owned everything. We had changed the system but we had not learned much about management and control. We also made some idealistic mistakes. But we had a lot more things to distribute than what we have today. Some said that Cuba had 'socialized poverty'. We answered, 'Yes, it is better to socialize poverty than to distribute the scarce wealth there is among a small minority that takes everything and leaves nothing for the rest of the people.'

Now more than ever, we are forced to distribute what we have as equitably as possible. However, there are now some privileges in our country. The reasons were inevitable for us: family remittances, tourism, opening to foreign investment in certain branches of the economy, something which has made our work in the political and ideological field more difficult, because the power of money is great; it must not be underestimated.

We have had to struggle a lot against all that. On the other hand, we had reached the conclusion that living in a glass case might be very pure but those who live that way, in total aseptic conditions, when they are out of them they may be finished off by a mosquito, an insect, a bacteria, just like many of the bacteria, parasites and viruses that the Spaniards brought over with them killed a great number of natives in this hemisphere. They lacked immunity. We said, 'We will learn to work under difficult conditions because, at the end of the day, virtue flourishes in the fight against vice'. Thus, we have had to face many problems under the present circumstances.

You had a period of huge incomes when the price of oil rose from 1.90 US dollars barrel in 1972 to 10.41 US dollars in 1974, to 13.03 US dollars in 1978, to 29.75 US dollars in 1979, until reaching the fabulous price of 39.69 US dollars in 1980. In the following years, from 1981 to 1985, the average price per barrel was 30.10 US dollars, a true stream of income in convertible currencies for this item. I know the story of what happened later, because I have a lot of friends who are professionals and every time I saw them I would ask about the situation, what was their salary then and what was their real income 10 years later. I have witnessed how that income dwindled year after year until today. I should not really make any other type of analysis. I always asked the Venezuelans those questions thinking about the country's situation.

These are not times of abundance – neither for Venezuela nor for the world. I am fulfilling an honest duty, a friend's duty, a brother's duty, by suggesting to you, who are a powerful intellectual vanguard, to meditate profoundly about these topics. We want to express to you our concern that this logical, natural and human hope, stemming from a sort of political miracle that has taken place in Venezuela might, in a short term, turn into disappointment and a weakening of such an extraordinary process.

I ask myself, I should and I do: what economic feats or miracles may be expected immediately with the prices of Venezuelan export commodities so low and oil at 9 US dollars a barrel? What with the lowest price in the last twenty-five years, a dollar which has a lot less purchasing power now, with a larger population, an enormous accumulation of social problems, an international economic crisis and a neo-liberally globalized world?

I cannot and should not say a word as to what we would do under such circumstances. I cannot. I am here as a guest, not as an adviser, an opinion giver or anything like that. I am simply meditating.

Allow me to say that I do not want to mention any, but there are some important countries whose situation is worse than yours, which I hope can overcome their difficulties.

Your situation is difficult, but not catastrophic. That would be our perception if we were in your place. I will tell you more with the same frankness. You cannot do what we did in 1959. You will have to be more patient than we were, and I am referring to that part of the people who want radical economic and social changes in the country.

If the Cuban Revolution had triumphed in a moment such as this, it would not have been able to sustain itself, I mean that same Cuban Revolution which has done all it has done. It emerged – and not because it was so calculated, but by a rare historic coincidence – fourteen years after World War II, in a bipolar world. We did not know a single Soviet citizen, nor did we ever receive a single bullet from the Soviets to carry out our struggle and our Revolution. Neither did we let ourselves to be guided by any type of political advice after the triumph, nor did anybody ever attempt it because we were very reluctant to that. We, Latin Americans in particular, do not like to be told what to do.

At that moment, of course, there was another powerful pole and so we anchored ourselves to that pole, which had come out of a great social revolution. It helped us to face the monster that cut off its oil and other vital supplies and reduced its imports of Cuban sugar bringing them down to zero as soon as we enforced a land reform law. Therefore, from one minute to the next, we were deprived of a market that had taken more than a century to build.

The Soviets, on the other hand, sold us oil. At world price, yes; to be paid in sugar, yes; at the world price of sugar, yes, but we exported our sugar to the USSR and we received oil, raw materials, food, and many other things. It gave us time to build a consciousness; it gave us time to sow ideas; it gave us time to create a new political culture. It gave us time! Enough time to build the strength that enabled us later to resist the most incredibly hard times.

All the internationalism that we have practised, which has already been mentioned, also made us stronger.

I do not think any country has endured more difficult circumstances. I am not at all boastful if I tell you, objectively, that no country in the world could have resisted. There might be some. If I think of the Vietnamese, I think the Vietnamese capable of any kind of resistance. I think the Chinese were equally capable of performing any kind of feat.

There are people with peculiar characteristics and conditions, deeply rooted cultures all their own, inherited from age-old ancestors, which give them enormous capacity for resistance. In the case of Cuba, it was a culture largely inherited from a world that became our enemy. We were completely surrounded by hostile regimes, hostile campaigns, a blockade and all sorts of economic pressures, which made our revolutionary tasks extremely difficult. We spent six years in war against the bandits employed by our powerful neighbour to implement its dirty war tactics. Also, many years fighting terrorists, assassination attempts . . . what else can I say, if not that it is a great privilege for me, after twenty years, to return to this place, so dear and unforgettable to me already. This is evidence of the inefficiency and failure of those who so often tried to accelerate the natural and inevitable process of life toward the end.

'you cannot kill ideas, you cannot kill ideas'

Now we can say the same thing a lieutenant said who took me prisoner in a forest near Santiago de Cuba in the early hours of dawn several days after the attack against the Moncada army garrison. We had made a mistake, there is always a mistake. We were tired of sleeping on the ground, over roots and stones, so we fell asleep in a makeshift hut covered with palm fronds. Then, we woke up with rifles pointed against our chests. It was a lieutenant, a black man, with a group of unmistakably bloodthirsty soldiers who did not know who we were. We had not been identified. At first, they did not identify us. They asked us our names. I gave a false name. Prudence, huh? Shrewdness? Perhaps it was intuition or maybe instinct. I can assure you that I was not afraid because there are moments in life when it is so, when you consider yourself as good as dead, and then it is rather your honour, your pride, your dignity that reacts.

If I had given them my name, that would have been it: tah, tah, tah! They would have done away with that small group immediately. A few minutes later they found some weapons nearby. These had been left behind by some comrades who were not in physical conditions to continue the struggle. Some of them were wounded and we had all agreed they should return to the city to turn themselves in to the judicial authorities. Only three of us were stayed, only three armed comrades! And we were captured the way I have just explained.

But that lieutenant, what an incredible thing! I have never told this story in detail publicly. This lieutenant was trying to calm down the soldiers but he could hardly stop them anymore. When they found the other comrades' weapons while searching the surroundings, they were infuriated. They had us tied up with their loaded rifles pointing at us. But the lieutenant moved around calming them down and repeating in a low voice: 'You cannot kill ideas, you cannot kill ideas'. What made this man say that?

He was a middle-aged man. He had taken some university courses and he had that idea in his head, and he felt the urge to express it in a low voice, as if talking to himself: 'You cannot kill ideas'. Well, when I look at this man and I see his attitude, in a critical moment when he was hardly able to keep those angry soldiers from firing, I get up and tell him: '*Lieutenantö*' – him alone, of course – 'I am so and so, first in command of the action. Seeing your chivalrous attitude, I cannot deceive you, I want you to know who you have taken prisoner.' And the man says, 'Do not tell anyone! Do not tell anyone!' I applaud that man because he saved my life three times in a few hours.

A few minutes later they were taking us with them and the soldiers were still very irritated. They heard some shots not far from there, got ready for combat and said to us, 'Drop down to the ground.' I remained standing and I said, 'I will not drop to the ground!' I thought it was some kind of trick to eliminate us, and I said, 'No.' I also told the lieutenant who kept insisting that we protected ourselves, 'I am not dropping to the ground, if they want to shoot let them shoot.' Then he says, listen to what he says, 'You boys are very brave.' What an incredible reaction!

I do not mean that he saved my life at that moment, but he had that gesture. After we reached a road, he put us in a truck and there was a major there who was very bloodthirsty. He had murdered many of our comrades and wanted the prisoners handed over to him. The lieutenant refused, said we were his prisoners and he would not hand them over. He had me sitting in the front seat of the truck. The major wanted him to take us to the Moncada but he did not hand us over to the major – there he saved our lives for the second time – nor did he take us to the Moncada.

He took us to the precinct, in the middle of the city, saving my life for the third time. You see, and he was an officer of that army we were fighting against. When the Revolution triumphed, we promoted him to captain and he became aide to the first President of the country after the triumph.

As that lieutenant said, ideas cannot be killed. Our ideas did not die, no one could kill them. And the ideas we sowed and developed during those thirty odd years until 1991 more or less, when the special period began, were what gave us the strength to resist. Without those years we had to educate, sow ideas, build awareness, instill feelings of solidarity and a generous internationalist spirit, our people would not have had the strength to resist.

I am speaking of things that are somewhat related to matters of political strategy. Very complicated things because they can be interpreted in different ways, and I know very well what I want to express. I have said that not even a Revolution like ours, which triumphed with the support of over 90 per cent of the population, a unanimous, enthusiastic backing, great national unity, a tremendous political force, would have been able to resist. We would not have been able to preserve the Revolution under the current circumstances of the globalized world.

I do not advise anyone to stop fighting, one way or another. There are many ways, and among them the action of the masses, whose role and growing strength are always decisive.

Right now, we ourselves are involved in a great combat of ideas, disseminating our ideas all over, that is our job. It would not occur to us today to tell anyone: 'Make a revolution like ours.' Because under the circumstances that we think we know quite well, we would not be able to suggest: 'Do what we did.' Maybe if we were in those times we would say: 'Do what we did.' But in those times the world was different and the experience was different. Now we are more knowledgeable, more aware of the problems and, of course, respect and concern for others should come first and foremost.

At the time of the revolutionary movements in Central America, when the situation had become very difficult because the unipolar world already existed and not even the Nicaraguan revolution could stay in power, and peace negotiations were begun, we were visited quite often because of the long friendship relations existing with Cuba, and we were asked our views. We would tell them: 'Do not ask our views about that. If we were in your place, we would know what to do, or we might be able to think what we should do. But you cannot give opinions to others when they are the ones who will have to apply opinions or criteria on matters as vital as fighting until death or negotiating. That decision only the revolutionaries of each country themselves can take. We will support whatever decision you make.

It was a unique experience, which I am telling in public for the first time, too. Everyone has his own options but no one has the right to convey to others his own philosophy on facing life or death. That is why I say that giving opinions is a very delicate matter.

This does not hold true for criteria, viewpoints and opinions about global issues that affect the planet, recommendable tactics and strategies of struggle. As citizens of the world and part of the human race, we have the right to clearly express our thoughts to those who want to hear, be they revolutionaries or not.

We learned a long time ago how our relations with the progressive and revolutionary forces must be. Here, before you, I limit myself to conveying ideas, reflections, concepts in keeping with our common condition of Latin American patriots because, I repeat, I see a new hour in Venezuela, an immovable and inseparable pillar of the history of our America. One has the right to trust one's own experience or viewpoint. Not because one is infallible or because one has not made mistakes, but because one has had the opportunity to take a 40 year-long course in the academy of the Revolution.

That is why I have told you that you do not have a catastrophic situation, but you do have a difficult economic situation which entails risks for that opportunity that is looming.

There have been very impressive coincidences. This situation in Venezuela has taken place at a critical moment in the integration of Latin America; a special moment in which those further to the South, in their endeavour for unity, need help from those in northern South America. In other words, they need your help. This has come at a moment in which the Caribbean countries need you. It has come at a moment when you can be the link, the bridge, the hinge whatever you want to call it, or a steel bridge between the Caribbean, Central America and South America.

Nobody like you is in a position to struggle for something so important and of so much priority at this difficult moment, as unity and integration, we might say, for the survival not only of Venezuela but of all the countries sharing our culture, our language and our race.

a united people ready to fight and win can be tremendously strong

Today more than ever we must be followers of Bolívar. Now more than ever we must raise the banner with the concept that humanity is our motherland, aware that we can only be saved if humanity is saved. We can only be free – and we are very far from being free – if and when humanity is free. If and when we achieve a really fair world, which is possible and probable, although from so much observing, meditating and reading, I have reached the conclusion that humanity has very little time left to achieve this.

This is not only my opinion, but the opinion of many other people I know. We recently held a Congress with 1,000 economists, 600 of them from different foreign countries, many eminent people, and we discussed the papers presented. Fifty-five papers were discussed and debated concerning these problems of the neo-liberal globalization, the international economic crisis, things that are happening. Because I should have added that, unfortunately, I am not much hopeful that the prices of your commodities will increase in the next two or three years.

Our nickel has also declined by half its price. You see, not so long ago it was 8,000 US dollars a ton, and now it is 4,000 US dollars. Two days ago, sugar was six and a half cents, a price that does not even cover production costs – the cost of fuel, spare parts, labour force, productive inputs and so on. That is a social, and not only an economic problem. Hundreds of thousands of workers live by the sugar mills and are very much attached to them with deeply rooted traditions of sugar production, traditions that have been transmitted from generation to generation. And we are not going to close their factories although, right now, we are facing losses in sugar production.

We have some resources. Tourism, developed mainly with our own resources, has gained momentum in these years and we have made several decisions that have proved effective. I am not going to explain how we have managed to achieve what I have already explained. But I should say that we did it avoiding shock policies, the famous therapies that have been so insensitively applied elsewhere.

What we applied were austerity measures consulted with all the people. Before submitting such measures to Parliament, they were submitted to the people and discussed with all the trade unions, the workers and the peasants. We discussed what to do with the price of a given item, what price to increase and why, what price not to increase and why. That was also discussed with all the students in hundreds of thousands of assemblies. Then the measures were submitted to the National Assembly and later they were taken back to the grassroots again. Every decision was previously discussed because nothing is implemented unless there is a consensus and that is something that cannot be achieved by force.

The wise men in the North believe or pretend to believe that the Cuban Revolution is forcibly sustained. They have not been clever enough to realize that in our country, a country educated in high revolutionary and humane concepts, that would be absolutely impossible. This is only achieved through consensus and nothing else; no one in the world can make it if it is not with the people's massive support and cooperation. But consensus has its own rules. We learned to create it, to maintain it and to defend it. A united people ready to fight and win can be tremendously strong. Once there was a small disturbance that was not essentially political. It was a moment when the United States was encouraging through every means illegal exits to its territory. Cubans received automatic residence rights, something the US does not grant to citizens of any other country in the world. This was an encouragement for anyone to make a raft stronger than the Kon-Tiki or to use a motor boat to travel to that rich country assisted by the Gulf stream. Many people have sport vessels. Others stole boats and were welcomed as heroes, with all honours.

In an incident related to a plan to steal a passenger boat in the port of Havana to create a migratory disorder there was some turmoil and some began to throw stones against some store windows. What did we do then? We have never used soldiers or policemen against civilians. We have never had a fire engine throwing powerful jets of water against people, as one can see in those images from Europe itself almost every day, nor people wearing masks as if ready for a trip to outer space. No, it is consensus that maintains and gives the Revolution its force.

That day, I remember, I was just getting to my office, it was about midday and I heard the news. I called my escorts, who were carrying weapons, and told them: 'We are heading for the disturbances. You are forbidden to use your weapons!' I really preferred to have someone shoot at me than using weapons in this type of situation, that is why I gave them categorical instructions and they dutifully went there with me.

How long did the disturbances last? Minutes, seconds perhaps. Most of the people were perched in their balconies. They were somewhat shocked, surprised. Some underclass were throwing stones. And, suddenly, I think even those who were throwing stones started to applaud, then the whole crowd moved and it was really impressive to see how the people react when it becomes aware of something that might harm the Revolution!

Well, I intended to get to the Havana City Museum where the city historian was. 'How might Leal be?' he was said to be besieged in the Museum. But some blocks away, near the sea wall a whole crowd was walking with us and there were no signs of violence. I had said: 'Not one unit should be moved, not one weapon, not one soldier.' If you trust the people and if you have the trust of that people, you do not have to use weapons ever. We have never used them in our country.

So what you need is unity, political culture and the conscious and militant support of the people. We built that through a long work. You Venezuelans, will not be able to create it in a few days, nor in a few months.

If instead of being an old friend, someone to whom you have made the great honour of receiving with affection and trust, if instead of being an old and modest friend – I say it candidly, since I am totally convinced of it – if it were one of the Venezuelan forefathers who was here; I dare say more, if it were that great and talented man who dreamt of the unity of Latin America who was here, talking to you right now, he would say: 'Save this process! Save this opportunity!'

I think you can be happy, and you will be happy, with many of the things you can do. Many already are at hand reach and depend on subjective factors and on very little resources. We have done that, but one cannot realistically think of abundant resources: with some adding and subtracting it would be easy to understand. Yes, you can find resources, and you can find them in many things to meet priority, fundamental, essential requirements. But you cannot dream that the Venezuelan society will now have the resources it once had, under very different circumstances. The world is in crisis, prices for raw materials are very low, and the enemy would try to make use of that.

Rest assured that our neighbours on the North are not at all happy with the process that is taking place in Venezuela, nor do they want it to succeed.

I am not here to sow discord, quite the opposite. I would recommend wisdom and caution, all the necessary caution, and no more than necessary. But you have to be skilled politicians. You will even need to be skilled diplomats. You should avoid frightening many people. Based on my own experience of many years, not on my own intelligence, I suggest that you subtract as few people as possible.

A transformation, a change, a revolution in the sense that word has today, when you look farther than the piece of land where you were born, when you think of the world, when you think of mankind, requires the participation of the people. Better add than subtract. Look, that lieutenant who commanded the platoon that took me prisoner was added to our cause, not subtracted from it. I took that man the way he was, and I have met some like him in my life. I would say I have met many like him.

It is true that the social environment, the social situation is the main factor in forging man's conscience. After all, I was the son of a landowner who had quite an extension of land in a country the size of Cuba, perhaps not so in Venezuela. My father had about 1,000 hectares of land of his own and 10,000 hectares of leased land that he exploited. He was born in Spain and as a young and poor peasant was enrolled to fight against the Cubans.

Recently, in an important American magazine someone trying to offend the Spaniards, annoyed because the Spaniards have increased their investments in Latin America, published a very harsh article against Spain. One could see from that article that they were really angry. They want everything for themselves. They do not want a Spanish peseta invested in these lands, let alone in Cuba, and among other things the article said that in spite of his attacks against imperialism, Fidel Castro admires the re-conquest. The article construed things as if it were a Spanish re-conquest. It was entitled 'In Search of the new El Dorado' and at one point in its furious attack it added that the Cuban ruler, the son of a Spanish soldier who fought on the wrong side during the war of independence, does not criticize the re-conquest.

I think about my father, who perhaps was 16 or 17 when he was enrolled over there and sent to Cuba as things were done in those days, and stationed in a Spanish fortified line. Could my father be really accused of fighting on the wrong side? No. In any case, he fought on the right side, he fought with the Spaniards. What do they want? That he should be an expert on Marxism, internationalism and a host of other things when he could barely read and write? I thought that they enlisted him and he fought on the right side. Those in the Yankee magazine are wrong. If he had fought on the Cuban side, he would have been on the wrong side because this was not his country. He knew nothing about it. He could not even understand what the Cubans were fighting for. He was a conscript. He was brought here as they brought other hundreds of thousands of people. When the war ended, he was repatriated to Spain and he came back to Cuba a little after to work as a farmhand.

Later he became a landowner. I was born and I lived in a large estate and it did not do me any harm. There I had my first friends. They were poor children of the place, the children of waged workers and modest peasants, victims all of the capitalist system. Later I went to schools that were more for the elite, but I came out unscathed, luckily. I really mean luckily. I had the fortune of being the son, and not the grandson of a landowner. If had I been the grandson of a landowner I would have probably been born and brought up in a city, among rich children, in a very high class neighbourhood, and I would have never had my utopian or Marxist communist ideas, nor anything similar.

No one is born a revolutionary, nor a poet or a warrior. It is the circumstances that make an individual or give him the opportunity of being one thing or the other.

If Columbus had been born a century before, no one would have heard of him. Spain was still under Arab occupation. If he had not been wrong and there had really been a path directly to China by sea without an unforeseen continent in between, he would have lasted fifteen minutes on the coast of China. Remember that the Spaniards conquered Cuba with just twelve horses and in those days the Mongols already had cavalries with hundreds of thousands of soldiers. See how things come to be.

I will not say anything about Bolívar, because he was born where he should, the day he should and in the way he should, that's it! I leave aside the scenario of what would have happened if he had been born a hundred years before or a hundred years later because that was impossible. [*Shouts from the audience: 'Che!'*]

Che? Che [Guevara] has been present here every second, in my words, speaking from here.

'today's dreams will be tomorrow's realities'

Now I will really finish. Some businessmen are waiting for me. How do I change my discourse? Well, I will tell them the same thing, honesty above all else. I believe that in this country there is a place for every honest person, for every sensitive person, for every person who can listen to the message of the homeland and of the times. I would say, the message of mankind is the one you should convey to your fellow countrymen and women.

I already told you about a meeting attended by 600 economists from various countries, many very intelligent people from the most diverse schools. We analysed all these problems in depth. We did not want a sectarian, leftist or rightist meeting. We even invited Mr Friedman but, of course, since he is now 82, he excused himself and said he could not come. We also invited Mr Soros to defend his points of view; the Chicago Boys; the supply side monetarists; the neo-liberals, because what we wanted was to discuss, and we discussed for five days beginning on a Monday and concluding on a Friday.

That meeting was the result of a suggestion I had made at a meeting of Latin American economists. Many things were being said, so I told them that with all the problems we are facing now, why could we not focus on the economic crisis and the problems of neo-liberal globalization? And so we did. Hundreds of papers were sent and 55 of them were chosen and all of them discussed. The others will be printed, the ones that were not discussed. They were very interesting, very educational and instructive. We were thinking of doing it every year. There is a forum in Davos, where I do not know how many representatives of transnationals and all the rich people in this world meet. Our small island can be a modest place where those who have no transnationals or anything of the sort can meet. But we are going to hold this meeting every year, based on the experience we had this time.

I had to close that meeting which lasted for five days. We had said: 'Look, there will be no guitars to start the meeting.' Because, as you know, meetings often start with guitars, with choruses . . .

Well, we had a chorus here, very well, a very good one. But I said: 'The meeting is to begin exactly on time to discuss the first paper.' And we did that for five days: morning, afternoon and evening sessions.

I had the task of closing the meeting and it was already midnight when I started talking. If you allow me, and it will only take some minutes, since it was very brief, I would like to repeat today what I said, because it covers very concisely the essence of many of the things I have said here.

'**Esteemed delegates, observers and guests,**

'You have honoured me by asking but I will not make a speech. I will limit myself to presenting a paper. I will do it in the style of a cablegram and it will mostly be a dialogue with myself.

'Month of July. Latin American and Caribbean Economists Meeting. Subject: Serious world economic crisis in sight. Need to convene an international conference. Focal point: Economic crisis and neo-liberal globalization.

'Extensive debate.

'Every school of thought represented.

'Exchange of arguments.

'Work done along these lines.

'Maximum possible reduction of expenses for everyone.

'Morning, afternoon and evening sessions.

'Exceptional seriousness and discipline have prevailed during these five days.

'We have all expressed ourselves in absolute freedom. We have made it. We are grateful.

'We have learned a lot from listening to you.

'A great variety and diversity of ideas. An extraordinary show of scholarly spirit and talent clearly and beautifully expressed.

'We all have our convictions.

'We can all influence each other.

'In the long run, we shall all reach similar conclusions.

'My deepest convictions: the incredible and unprecedented globalization under discussion is a product of historical evolution, a fruit of human civilization achieved in a very short period of time, in no more than 3000 years of the long presence of our ancestors on the planet. They were already a completely developed specie. The man of today is not more intelligent than Pericles, Plato or Aristotle, and we do not know as yet if he is intelligent enough to solve today's extremely complex problems. We are betting on his doing it. That is what we have dealt with at our meeting.

'A question: is it a reversible process? My answer, the one I give to my self, is No.

'What kind of globalization have we today? A neo-liberal globalization, that is what many of us call it. Is it sustainable? No. Will it be able to subsist for long? Absolutely, no. Is it a matter of centuries? Categorically, no. Will it last only decades? Yes, only decades. But sooner rather than later it will cease to exist.

'Do I believe myself to be a sort of prophet or fortune-teller? No. Do I know much about economics? No. Hardly anything. To make this statement it is enough to know how to add up, subtract, multiply and divide – something children learn in grammar school.

'How will such transition take place? We do not know. Will it be through violent revolutions or devastating wars? That seems unlikely, irrational and suicidal. Will it be through deep and catastrophic crisis? Unfortunately, this is most likely, almost inevitable and it will happen through many different ways and forms of struggle.

'What kind of globalization will it be? It cannot but be supportive, socialist, communist or whatever you want to call it.

'Does nature, and the human species with it, have much time left to survive in the absence of such change? Very little time. Who will be the builders of that new world? The men and women who inhabit our planet.

'Which will be their basic weapons? Ideas will be, and consciousness. Who will sow them, cultivate them and make them invincible? You will. Is it a utopia, just one more dream among so many others? No, because it is objectively inevitable and there is no alternative to it. It has been dreamt of before, only perhaps too early. As the most visionary of the sons and daughters of this island, José Martí, said: 'Today's dreams will be tomorrow's realities.'

'I have concluded my presentation. Thank you.'

I am sorry

I have been so imposing and I promise you that in forty years, when you invite me again, I will be more concise.

You were lucky I did not include the famous booklet. You know what it was? The paper on the Synod in Rome, published in Mexico. I was not going to read it, but much of what I underlined when reading this apostolic exhortation coincided with many of the ideas I expressed here. I was going to use it as an evidence that much of what is being thought today in the world on the calamitous existing system does not only come from leftist sources, not only comes from political sources. Arguments, expressions or contentions condemning poverty, injustices, inequalities, neo-liberalism, the squandering of consumer societies and many other social and human disasters resulting from the present economic order imposed on the world also come from institutions that cannot be suspected of Marxism, such as the Roman Catholic church. Many other Christian churches think likewise.

Perhaps it would have been best to come with this paper and read what I had underlined. That way you would have been able to leave four hours and a half earlier.

Thank you very much.

THE BATTLE FOR SOVEREIGNTY IS A BATTLE FOR CULTURE TOO

Esteemed ministers and
cultural leaders in the countries of Latin America or Ibero-America,
distinguished guests, dear delegates to the first International Congress on
Culture and Development,

During four days those of you who took part in the Congress
have worked hard. Happily, your efforts coincided with the ministers' and
culture leaders' two-days meeting – on the 10th and 11th – preceding the
Ibero-American Summit Conference to be held in the month of November.
We have tried to be informed of what you have discussed and what the
debates have been like.

It seems to me that the organizers are satisfied with the results of
both meetings.

Among the subjects discussed – and undoubtedly there were
many and of great value – some caught my particular attention. I find
they are among the subjects related to culture and politics that I mostly
appreciate. For example, the need for states to promote a correct policy of
environmental education; the importance of history to convey values and
defend the peoples' identity; the need to reject colonialist or hegemonic

models; the advisability of avoiding damages to the national identity from tourism; the necessity to meditate on the current world, to build a public awareness and to transmit ideas which I consider of basic importance; the urgent need to foster a true revolution of man's ethic through his education and the implementation of the right cultural policies. This is really the first time that I see this last subject so clearly formulated.

Finally, there is an item 12, which I do not know if absolutely everybody will agree with but at least I do, and it reads: 'The capitalist economy cannot guarantee the prospective development of humanity because it does not take into account the cultural and human losses that result from its own expansion'. I would go a little bit further and say that not only does it not guarantee the prospective development of humanity but that, as a system, it puts at risk its very existence.

You urged me to say a few words the day that the Congress opened and I touched on an essential point related to the transfer of ideas.

I do not know how much discussion there has been on the ways to implement that principle. I do know, however, that as a fundamental part of the integration policy that is up for debate, you have raised the need for culture to be given a priority over the other objectives of that integration.

We feel that, united we would be worth the sum of many and very rich cultures. In this token, when we think about Our Americas, as José Martí called it, the Americas down from the Rio Bravo [Rio Grande] – although it should have been from the Canadian border because that portion also belonged to our Americas until an insatiable expansionist neighbour seized the whole territory of the west of what is today the United States of America – it is that integration which I have in mind, but including the Caribbean nations.

The Caribbean nations are still not present in these Ibero-American Summit conferences. Fortunately, all Latin American and Caribbean countries will, for the first time, meet with the European Union in Rio de Janeiro on the 28th and 29th of this month. So, the family is already growing although, in general, the Caribbean nations have been the last of the forgotten as we, Latin Americans, also were and still are forgotten.

a free unity of all cultures in a truly just world

The sum of all our cultures would make up one enormous culture and be a multiplication of our cultures. Integration should not adversely affect, but rather enrich, the culture of every one of our countries.

In this context, when we talk about unity we still do so in a narrow framework. But I like to go beyond that. I believe in the unity of all the countries in the world, in the unity of all the peoples in the world and in a free unity, a truly free unity. I am not thinking of a fusion but of a free unity of all cultures in a truly just world, in a truly democratic world, in a world where it would be possible to apply the kind of globalization that Karl Marx talked about in his time and that [Pope] John Paul II talks about today when he speaks of the globalization of solidarity.

We still need a good definition of what the globalization of solidarity means. If we take this thought to its final consequences we will realize that item 12 is a reality because I wonder if the capitalist system can guarantee the globalization of solidarity. No one speaks about the 'globalization of charity', which would be very good in the meantime, but let us hope the day will come when charity is unnecessary. That will be the day when the sentiments of solidarity become universal and the spirit of solidarity goes global.

I say this to make it clear that I am in no way a narrow nationalist or a chauvinist. I hold man in a higher concept and cherish more ambitious dreams for the future of the human species, which has gone through so much hardship to end up being what it is today, and accumulated such knowledge as it has today, while still not deserving the description of a truly human species. What we presently have is still very far from that but, perhaps, the further it seems, the closer it actually is, since this humanity is going through a colossal crisis and it is only from colossal crises that great solutions may come.

That is what history has been teaching us so far, up to this very moment when the real globalization, which was not even mentioned a few years ago, has been made possible and inevitable by the enormous advances in science, technology and communications. People communicate with one another in a matter of seconds, wherever they are.

Suffice it to say that it is more difficult for me to communicate with our Minister of Foreign Affairs here than with our Ambassador in the United Nations. The Ambassador there has a cellular phone and even if he is in the meeting room beside his colleague, the US Ambassador – with an empty seat between them – he can talk over the phone. Just today, when the phone connection was made and I asked where he was – whether in the mission, at home or in the United Nations – he said: 'I am in the car.' I said: 'In the car! But I hear you so well!' He said: 'Yes, we have stopped at the traffic light now.' And we continued talking for several more minutes. It is incredible, really.

Technological advances explain the accuracy of the famous satellites guiding the missiles and the smart weapons which are not so smart that they fail disturbingly often – that is, if they actually fail unintentionally.

The incident with the Chinese embassy [in Belgrade] seemed so strange, so bizarre; when in trying to explain it they said the problem was that they had been bombing guided by some old outdated maps. So, due to some outdated maps a bomb could have fallen here too, in this meeting room.

Money moves rapidly, too, and speculative operations with currencies are carried out at great speed for a trillion dollars every day; and they are not the only speculative operations taking place, nor is it only with currencies they speculate.

At the time of Maghellan, it took I do not know how many months to go round the world and now it can be done in barely 24 hours.

Me too, I went round the world not long ago, stopping off in Denmark, China, Vietnam, Japan, Canada and back to Havana. I then began playing with the numbers and doing some calculations and I realized that flying East, on a faster plane than mine, it is possible to leave China early on Monday morning and arrive in Havana on Sunday afternoon.

We have seen the world change in a few decades.

an awesome offensive against sovereignty

If you do not mind I will introduce an issue, just like you have introduced many others, and I would call it 'Culture and Sovereignty'.

I will rely on concrete facts and I am not talking theory or philosophy but things that we can all see, that even a near-sighted person can see: namely, that there can be no culture without sovereignty. [Minister of Culture] Abel [Prieto] outlined how a handful of brilliant personalities succeeded in saving the national culture from American neocolonialism and hegemonism in Cuba.

Another country has more merit than we do: Puerto Rico, which has been a Yankee colony for 100 years now, but neither their language nor culture have been destroyed. It is admirable!

Of course, imperialism has today much more powerful means to destroy cultures, to impose other cultures and homogenize cultures – much more powerful means. Perhaps, at this moment, it can be more influential in 10 years than it was in the past 100 years. However, the example I gave you sheds some light on the peoples' capacity to resist and on the value of culture. The Puerto Ricans were deprived of all sovereignty and, despite everything, they have resisted.

Although it is possible to find examples to show that there can be culture, or that a certain degree of culture can be preserved without sovereignty, what is inconceivable or unimaginable in today's world and toward the future is the existence of sovereignty without culture.

While you, Congress delegates, ministers and government leaders of culture in Ibero-America were here yesterday involved in your debates, a great battle was being fought at the United Nations for sovereignty and we would say a major battle for culture, too. Yes, because I say that, today, the means in the hands of those who dominate the world economically and almost politically are much more powerful than they ever were.

That great battle had to do with the Security Council meeting which discussed a draft resolution on the war unleashed against Yugoslavia, basically against Serbia. In my view, it was a historic battle because imperialism and its allies – or better still, imperialism and those who support it against their own best interests – are waging a massive struggle against the principle of sovereignty, an awesome offensive against sovereignty.

We could see this coming. After the collapse of the socialist camp, the USSR disintegrated and a single superpower remained in the world. It was noticeable that that superpower – of well known origins whose diabolical methods and principles are also very well known – could not refrain from trying to use all its vast power to impose its standards and its interests on the world, carefully at first and then by increasingly stark means.

We are already looking at an imperialism that is using all its might and force to sweep away anything that stands in its way and culture is one of those things very much in its way. They are the owners of the vast majority of the communication networks, that is, 60 per cent of the world communication networks and of the most powerful and unrivalled television channels. And, they have the almost absolute monopoly of the films shown in the world.

It can be said that France, which is fighting an almost heroic battle to preserve its culture as much as possible against the United States' cultural invasion, is the only country in Europe, that I know of, where the American films shown account for less than 50 per cent of the total. In the other countries of the Old Continent, it is above 50 per cent. In some of them it can be 60, 65, 70 and even 80 per cent. As for television serials, it is 60, 70, 80 and 90 per cent, so that about 70 per cent of the television serials shown and 75 per cent of the video cassettes distributed are from the United States; these figures that you must have heard before. [The French journalist] Ramonet writes about those figures. It is an almost absolute monopoly.

There are major Latin American countries where 90 per cent of the films and serials shown come from the United States and you know the characteristics of what comes there. Very little material comes from Europe, so in those aspects there is a total cultural colonization by the United States.

It goes without saying that, in our case, it is extremely difficult to find films of some moral and cultural value. How do we escape from films that show violence, sex and the Mafia almost exclusively? How do we escape from so many alienating and poisonous films that they distribute throughout the world? It becomes difficult for us, for our television practically without commercials, as I said to you, to find films to show on weekends; and people are often critical of what is shown. On the other hand, they are copies because we should say, in all sincerity, that as we were blockaded and all our imports prevented, we found ourselves forced to copy.

Some things are easy to copy, including films, and I think that the comrades in our prestigious ICAIC [Cuban Films Institute] in the early years – and rightly so, it is a historical merit – specialized in copying US films. Then, there were some good ones. I mean, in the past there used to be more good American and European films. They were worth watching.

The commercial spirit has so pervasively penetrated culture as to become overwhelming. Which country in Europe can spend 300 million US dollars or more on a film? Which country in Europe can make profits of 500 million US dollars, or even 1.2 billion US dollars trading on paraphernalia related to a film? Those are companies that exploit everything, and the sales of goods associated to an expensive and highly publicized film actually give them higher profits than the screening of the film.

Actually, those films can cover all their costs and produce high profits in the United States market alone. Therefore, as you can easily understand, they can sell the films much more cheaply anywhere in Europe or the world. Who can compete with them?

Still, those European countries, some of them in a real cultural shock and other relatively indifferent to the phenomenon, who with their unity and integration expect to develop their economic, technological, scientific and cultural possibilities – practically as a necessity for survival – even those countries support the imperialist policy. They are supporting a policy aimed at sweeping away the principles of sovereignty. And it is not the case of very small countries, small islands or very poor underdeveloped nations whose per capita Gross Domestic Product is 200 or 300 US dollars a year, but rather countries whose per capita GDP is 20, 25, 30 and even 40,000 US dollars.

They, of course, are giving up national sovereignty to the extent that they are uniting, opening borders, applying the free circulation of capital, of workers, of technicians and creating common institutions that provide advantages only for the European countries. The South countries must arrive in little boats and enter illegally.

a piece of paper that circulates as if it were gold

Those countries are giving up their national currencies, and with good logic, in order to adopt a common currency. That is different from adopting a foreign currency governed by the US Federal Reserve System, which is tantamount to annexing the country to the United States.

What would become of us, who have, at least, demonstrated that it is possible to resist a double blockade and such a difficult period as we have gone through during these years? How would that have been possible without our own currency? To this I would add, as in passing, that we have revalued our currency seven times. From 1994, when one US dollar bought 150 pesos, to 1999 or the end of 1998 – let us say almost five years; the whole of 1994 should be counted – we have revalued the currency seven times. Today, one US dollar can only buy about 20 pesos. No country has done that, I tell you. None!

The formulas of the [International] Monetary Fund, all the recipes that it imposes and that you know so well, where do they lead? Sometimes, through privatization or savings the countries are able to accumulate major reserves to protect their currency, but then, in a number of days or weeks, they lose everything. We have seen that happen in a matter of days. We neither have nor need those enormous reserves. Other countries have them and lose them.

There is only one country – one single country in the world! – that does not even need a reserve because it prints the banknotes that circulate throughout the world; the country that, as we have said on other occasions, first converted gold into paper by unilaterally suspending the free conversion of its banknotes and which changed the gold in its reserves for the paper currency that it printed – a currency accepted by everybody for its equivalent value in gold. Later, then, it converted the paper into gold, the miracle dreamt of by the alchemists of the Middle Ages. In other words, they print a piece of paper that circulates as if it were gold. I am explaining the phenomenon in a simple way, although the procedure is more complicated than that.

They use Treasury bonds and apply different mechanisms. But, in essence, the fact is that they can afford it because they print the currency that circulates worldwide, they print the banknotes kept as a reserve in the banks of every country in the world. They print the paper, they buy with it and the others keep the paper – a large part of it, not all of it, of course. Therefore, they are the ones who print the world's reserve currency.

That is one of the reasons for the emergence of the euro. Let us say that it is an attempt to survive against that privilege and against that monetary power so that no speculator can come along and do to any

European country as they did to the United Kingdom, France, Spain and others when their currencies were devalued after they fell prey to enormous speculative operations. Actually, when some American megamillionaire wolves get together, no country can resist their speculative attacks. The pound sterling, a currency queen not so long ago, was brought to its knees in a matter of days.

That can give you an idea of what I mean. That country – well, there is hardly any need to say it – is the United States of America, the only one protected. Others, faced with the continuous and incessant devaluations, crises, catastrophes and flights of capital, in their desperation begin considering the idea of suppressing their national currencies and adopting the US dollar which is governed by the United States Federal Reserve.

Now, could our country survive if we had such a system? That is, if our currency were the US dollar and this country blockaded and unable to acquire dollars, were to buy the peasants' products – chicken, eggs, mangoes – in US dollars, could this country exist? Based on what we have had to go through and what we have learnt, we realize that in our conditions, if we did not have our very modest peso, which we have revalued, as I said, seven times, we would not have been able to revalue in the slightest. Practically all the schools would have been closed here while not a single one has been closed, and all the hospitals while not a single one has been closed. On the contrary, in this special period, we have increased the country's medical staff, especially the doctors working in the community but also those working in the hospitals by a figure that comes to approximately 30,000 new doctors. All this despite our great economic difficulties, lack of resources and often even of medicines, although we have the basic ones.

Today, a newspaper reported that in a central province of the country, not in the capital but in Villa Clara, infant mortality in children under one year was 3.9 per 1,000 live births. If we consider Washington, the United States capital, for example, its infant mortality rate is four or five times higher than in the Villa Clara province. There is one area, the Bronx, where it is 20 per 1,000 live births and other places in the United States where it is 30 per 1,000.

Our national average of infant mortality is lower than the United States national average by at least two or three percentage points. They are at perhaps 10 or 11 and our hope this year is to reduce it to 7 per 1,000. Last year, it was 7.1.

Needless to say that it is due to the efforts made that not a single day-care centre has been closed. Not a single family doctor's office has been closed. The number of doctor's offices has increased by many thousands during the special period. We have been able to do this, of course, because there is a revolution, there is a united people, there is a spirit of sacrifice and there is an extensive political culture.

When we speak about culture we do not forget the political culture. It is one of the sectors whose development is badly needed and which is very much lacking in the world. It is impossible to believe or imagine that an average person in the United States has a higher political culture than a Cuban or a European. I admit that Europeans have a higher political culture than Americans but, in general, Europeans do not have a higher political culture than Cubans. That is for sure. You could even have a contest to compare the European average political knowledge and the Cuban average, a contest between people who unfortunately live alienated by millions of things, and people who do not live like that.

In our Latin American countries, sometimes necessity and poverty help in the development of a political culture higher than in those very rich countries that do not suffer the calamities that we do. That is why, in the Latin American Teachers' Congresses held in Cuba with thousands of teachers in attendance, they constantly speak of the horrors of the neo-liberalization that cuts off their budgets; and, in the medical Congresses they do likewise, as in the students' Congresses or any congress for that matter, because they see it every day and they are conscious of it. Of course, awful things happen in Latin America that have not been seen for quite some time in Europe where the unemployed enjoy benefits that, according to some, allow them to vacation abroad for 15 days and more a year.

Where none of that exists, people suffer much more. We have more fertile ground to become politically cultured. In our case, we also have the experience accumulated by the country in very difficult battles against imperial aggression and in very great difficulties; and difficulties make good fighters.

But, all that notwithstanding, we could have done of what I am telling you if we did not have a national currency that helps us to redistribute, and also many free services.

Of course, you compare it with the US dollar and there comes the misleading formula of the exchange rate between the US dollar and the Cuban peso in the exchange bureau. And, if they say that it is 20 to 1, then somebody earning 300 Cuban pesos is said to earn 15 US dollars. If it was in New York, to those 15 US dollars you would have to add 1,000 to 1,500 US dollars to pay the rent, another 500 to pay for public health services – this is about 2,000 already – another 500 or 1,000 for education, depending on the educational level because there are university courses there that cost 30,000 dollars a year. Then add some 750 dollars more for the free education given to children, adolescents and young people here and the total could be some 2,750 US dollars, plus 15 that would be 2,765 dollars. All this is very misleading, is it not?

If you take into account that all children in Cuba up to the age of seven receive a litre of milk for 25 cents of a Cuban peso, then this would be a child or a family that is paying only 1.3 (1.25) cents of a US dollar out of the supposed 15 US dollars, for a litre of milk, and similarly for other essential food. Unfortunately, there is not enough food but there is a certain amount that, measured in dollars, is bought at a minute price.

If you go to our stadium, you can watch an important baseball match for 50 cents or one peso at most. If you go to Baltimore, where our team played the US team, of the 45,000 fans there, the ones who paid the least paid 10 US dollars and the ones who paid the most paid 35. To watch a similar performance a hundred times, a cuban pays a maximum of 100 pesos. An American must pay 3,500 dollars. The same applies to a lot of other activities and services. But our system, with all those characteristics, could not have had such achievements without a national currency.

Well, so much for this long disquisition on the importance of a national currency and the delirious things crossing the minds of those considering the removal of the national currency.

we do not tend to worry about anything

There in Europe, when they talk about sovereignty, they cannot have the same concept as we do. They are uniting and giving up many of the attributes of the nation state to a supranational state, to a supranational community. Other countries elsewhere in the world should do that and we, Latin Americans, should do that, too. If not, we will not advance even three yards. In fact, we will go backwards more yards every year if we do not integrate. In the light of what is happening in the world, it is not something to preach but rather to build an awareness about, to transmit a basic idea.

Actually, there is a very close powerful neighbour who wants to integrate us into it. Of course, this is to have access to our natural resources and the cheap labour of hundreds of millions of Latin Americans producing jeans, shoes, T-shirts, handicrafts that are very labour-intensive. Meanwhile, they keep the cutting-edge industries and the brain drain continues. Right now, they are talking about hiring 200,000 highly qualified foreign workers for their electronic industries, preferably Latin Americans. And so, they take away those highly qualified people that you train in the universities, the most scientifically talented. They give visas to them all right. These do not need to become wetbacks or illegal immigrants.

If there is a good artist, an excellent artist who can be exploited commercially, he is coaxed to go there. They cannot coax a great writer like Garcia Marquez because Garcia Marquez might be coaxing them. At the very least, with the high value of his works he might take a substantial part of the banknotes they print. Actually, a good writer can work in his own country, he does not need to emigrate; but in many areas of the arts it is not the same and they are coaxing the best talents to go there; many of them, at least. A man like Guayasamin could not be bought, not with all the money printed by the Federal Reserve. There are men who cannot be seduced with any money, men and women – I rather add those two words than be accused of gender discrimination – and we have them here. We have them here! I do not need to mention names, they are humble men and women who are worth more than all the gold in the world. That is a fact.

I am explaining all this because they can help understand these phenomenon of sovereignty, this battle. Because there are so many lies, so much demagogy, so much confusion and so many methods devised to disseminate them that an enormous effort should be made at constant clarification. If some things are not understood, the rest cannot be understood.

They talk about flight of capital, about volatile capital such as the short-term loans, as if those were the only kind of volatile capital. In any

Latin American country, the volatile capital suddenly goes. But, alongside the volatile capital goes all the money saved by the country's savers' because if some people withdraw their money for fear of a devaluation or so, the others rush to the bank, change it for US currency and transfer it to the US banks where the interest rate is higher or lower, depending on the situation.

So, all the Latin American and Caribbean money is volatile capital. Let us be well aware of this. Volatile capital is not limited to those short-term loans with a high interest rate that are then quickly withdrawn by the owners when faced with a risky situation. Any money can become volatile, except for Cuban money; there is no way our money can become volatile. If they want to take it away we shall be delighted. The liquidity would decrease and the value of the peso would increase.

Now the Europeans are uniting. They do it to compete with their competitor. They talk about being partners, but the United States does not want to be anybody's partner. At any rate, our neighbour wants to be a privileged partner. It constantly takes measures against Europe: banning the export of cheese for such a reason or other, or whatever other meat products because they use a certain fodder. They are always fabricating pretexts. Right now, because of the banana and a resolution from the World Trade Organization which is not unbiased, they have punished European exports for a total of about 500 million dollars. They take measures every day or threaten to take them. They are always wielding that weapon. Indeed, it is very clear to anybody who does a little thinking that Europe must compete very hard with them.

We welcome this Caribbean and Latin American meeting with the European Union that I previously mentioned. It is good and it is convenient. I think that it is convenient for Europe, it is convenient for the Caribbean and for Latin America as well. And let us hope that the euro is strengthened. It has now dropped a little. It is enduring the consequences of that adventurous and genocidal war – to call it by its true name.

It suits us that there is another reserve currency, so that there are two and not just one in the world. If only there were three! It suits us that there is more than one strong and stable currency. I hope that, among the many historical acts of madness committed in this hemisphere we do not end up adopting the US dollar as a circulation currency. It is a currency entirely managed from the United States by the Federal Reserve and they are not going to accept any Latin American representative there. Because, if they were willing to accept in their Federal Reserve System a representative for each Latin American country, even we would send them one, if we were allowed to, of course.

Obviously, that is a utopia. Of course, they are not going to welcome anybody, not even from the richer and more developed countries with a higher GDP, not even from Brazil, Argentina or Mexico, to mention the largest fraternal countries of Latin America. They are never going to accept our representatives in their Reserve System. The Latin American and Caribbean destiny is in danger but everything is not lost, far from it, we can still fight.

I hope you understand, European comrades, that the concept of sovereignty cannot be the one openly and shamelessly defended yesterday by a European representative for the first time since ideas began to be debated and doctrines developed against sovereignty. Europe, in general, is quite committed to that anti-sovereignty doctrine promoted by the imperialism of the superpower.

This explains that a European country – whose ambassador spoke at the United Nations in a way nobody had ever spoken there – could regard as anachronistic the United Nations Charter and the principle of sovereignty and non-intervention, something fundamental in international law. Those who so express themselves have practically renounced sovereignty and will enjoy, in the near future, a simple national autonomy within a supranational state, with a supranational parliament and a supranational executive.

Even now, as a reward for his glorious wartime exploits and forgetting those who died and the millions who have suffered and will keep those wounds for life, they have created the position of European Minister of Foreign Affairs; a prize for an outstanding character who seriously believes that he is what he is not and who acts like he really is. I mean the great Marshall and Secretary-General of NATO.

Do you not know who that is? Have you ever heard of him? He was a minister of culture in a European country. He is Javier Solana. Did you not know that he was a minister of culture? I met him at an Ibero-American summit in Spain, he awaited me at the airport and I chatted with him for a few minutes as protocol demands. He was at the time a peaceful minister who actively participated in anti-NATO demonstrations.

Today, he is the Secretary-General of NATO and a Field Marshal. He must really be at least a Field Marshal to give orders to the American generals. Now, they are making him a sort of European foreign minister.

Our comrades are asked by the press: are you not worried that they have named him Europe's Minister of Foreign Affairs? We, in fact, do not tend to worry about anything, nor do we exchange principles for interests or convenience. But we might answer that we would rather have him as a Minister of Foreign Affairs than as a NATO Field Marshal. I do not know what his power will be as a minister of Foreign Affairs but we know only too well the power that he claims as a NATO Secretary-General.

We have all the statements he has made, both before and during the war, and I know few people as attached to the doctrine of violence who use such a threatening style, with such a merciless and tough language. Obviously, he has a very great responsibility which he assumed when he formally ordered US General [Wesley] Clark, head of the NATO military forces in Europe, to start bombing at such and such an hour and at such and such a point, after the NATO countries had given their Secretary-General the power to start the war when, in his view, the diplomatic procedures had been exhausted.

In his capacity as Secretary-General he issued orders and made statements almost constantly during more than 70 days of brutal bombings. They were all threatening, arrogant, abusive, almost cynical statements. Then, after the Security Council's meeting yesterday he issued the last of his assumed orders: the cessation of the bombings. All this with the corresponding theatrical overtones.

How obedient those American generals! A model of discipline such as history had never seen! They immediately attack or they immediately cease to attack because a distinguished ex-Minister of Culture gives the order.

Can the countries of the European Union have the same concept of sovereignty as Mexico, Cuba, the Dominican Republic or any small Caribbean island, like a Central American country or like Venezuela, Colombia, Ecuador, Peru, Brazil, Argentina or a South-East Asian country like Indonesia, Malaysia or the Philippines? Can they have the same concept as the vast majority of countries in the world which are dismembered?

there were men who dreamt

When we are all integrated in a Latin America and Caribbean union, our concept of sovereignty will be different. We will have to give up a lot of those principles to obey the laws and the administration or the decisions of a supranational state.

Moreover, a Marxist can never be a narrow national chauvinist. A Marxist can be a patriot, which is different, and love his or her homeland, which is different, too.

A long time before today, there were men who dreamt, like [Simon] Bolívar almost two hundred years ago, of a united Latin America. There were men like Martí who, more than a hundred years ago, dreamt of a united Latin America. At that time, when Bolívar proclaimed his dreams, Latin America was not made up of free independent countries, not yet.

In fact, the first independent country following the United States of America was Haiti, a country that provided material assistance to Bolívar in his struggle for Latin American independence and which also contributed, with its ideas and exchanges, to consolidate Bolívar's consciousness about the impossibility to defer the slaves' emancipation, which was not attained after the first triumphant independence movement in Venezuela.

As you know, there was in the United States a struggle for independence and a declaration of principles in 1776. But, it was only after almost 90 years and a bloody war that the emancipation of slaves was formally declared. Of course, the slaves situation was often worse off afterwards since they were no longer any master's property, they were no longer their owners' assets; so, if they died, the former masters did not lose a dime. Previously, if a slave died, his or her master lost what the slave had cost him in the infamous auction. Later, as it was the case here too, and everywhere, they were practically worse off.

In Latin America, slavery as a system disappeared at a much earlier stage than in the United States. There were men who dreamt about those things. There were men who, for the creation of a great, united and strong republic dreamt that each of our current countries, without renouncing their national sentiments, would lay down their prerogatives or aspirations to the separate national independence of each of them.

There were not even independent states when Bolívar dreamt of a united, big and powerful Latin American state based on our similarities, such as no other group of countries in the world have in terms of language, ethnic groups of similar ancestry, religious beliefs and general culture.

Religion is also a part of culture. When we see the invasion of Latin America by fundamentalist sects – these things are known, these ideas emerged during the Cold War – I wonder about this invasion that wants to divide us into a thousand pieces. Why is there this fundamentalist invasion, by hundreds, even thousands of religious denominations that are not at all ecumenical, that are different from the traditional Christian religious denominations which have an increasing ecumenical spirit?

When I was a student there was nothing ecumenical about them. Really, when the Pope visited us, in my welcoming speech, I praised the current ecumenical spirit of his church. I recalled that it was not like that in my early youth, from first grade until I graduated from high school when I studied in Catholic schools. As a rule, I was a boarding student except for very short periods when I was a day pupil. Relations among the traditional churches have changed a lot since then.

Now I wonder, why do they want to fragment us with this invasion of thousands of non-unitary sects? As we understand it, in Latin America common religious beliefs constitute an important element of culture, identity and integration. It is not that there has to be a single church – far from it – but pro-unity churches, ecumenical churches. Such elements should be preserved.

We, Latin Americans, have many more things in common than the Europeans. Until not long ago, for centuries, they were warring against each other. There was one war that they called the Hundred Years War, and wars of every kind: religious, national, ethnic wars. Those who know a bit of history know that only too well.

The Europeans have transcended all that because they have become aware of the importance of unity. It must be said, really, that the Europeans became conscious – their politicians, in general, did – of the need to unite and to integrate and for around 50 years they have been working to that end. We have hardly even started.

The United Nations Charter and the principles of sovereignty are absolutely indispensable and crucial for the vast majority of peoples in the world, especially for the smallest and weakest who are still not integrated into any strong supranational grouping in the current stage of extraordinarily uneven political, economic and social development of the human community.

who trained the torturers?

The United States, captain and leader of the doctrines fostered by NATO, wants to sweep away the foundations of national sovereignty. It simply wants to take possession of the markets and natural resources of the Third World countries including those that were part of the former Soviet Union, like Azerbaijan, Uzbekistan, Turkmenistan and others, while it is already almost the master of the great oil reserves of the Caspian sea. It wants to play the role of a new Roman worldwide super-empire which, of course, will last much less than the Roman Empire and the reach of its ambitions and its clumsiness; and it will meet with universal resistance.

Nonetheless, it is preparing for the development, consolidation and exercise of a boundless empire. Some American analysts and writers from the same group as Ramonet – and Ramonet himself – denounce the cultural invasion, the almost total dominion over the mass media and the cultural monopoly they are trying to impose on the world, thus showing the way. The empire's most fervent theoreticians consider culture to be the nuclear weapon of the twenty-first century. But, there is no need to be so well informed to realize this. It can be seen clearly in everything they do and in the way they do it.

The empire's pretexts? Ah, humanitarian reasons! Human rights is one of the reasons they give for which it is necessary to liquidate sovereignty and internal conflicts that must be resolved with 'smart' bombs and missiles.

Whose proposal is this? Looking back, recalling what happened in our hemisphere in the past few decades, who fathered all the *coups d'état*? Who trained the torturers in the most sophisticated techniques? Who was responsible for there being relatively small countries where more than 100,000 persons vanished and a total of about 150,000 were killed? Or the fact that, in other nations, tens of thousands of men and women had a similar fate? I am talking here only about people who vanished after horrible torture. Who trained the sinister culprits? Who armed them? Who supported them? How can they now claim that national sovereignty must be removed in the name of human rights?

A few years ago, they killed four million Vietnamese by dropping millions of tons of explosives on a country that was 15,000 or 20,000 kilometers away. For a long time they kept fiercely bombing with the result of four million people dead and a large number disabled for life. Now, they are asking that sovereignty be removed in the name of human rights.

In Angola, for example, who armed UNITA, which, for more than 20 years, massacred entire villages and killed hundreds of thousands of Angolans? We know very well who did it because we were there a long time supporting the Angolan people against the South African racists. They are still killing there and their favourite leader has hundreds of millions of US dollars in the banks – I do not know who launders the money – part of which is used to buy weapons, much to the pleasure of arms manufacturers. He controls extensive areas that are very rich in diamonds and has a personal fortune of hundreds of millions of US dollars.

Likewise, there has been no repressive government in the world that the United States would not support. How could the apartheid regime have seven nuclear weapons? They had seven when we were there, on the Namibian border and, the United States intelligence service, which knows everything, did not know about it! Did it not know? And, how did those weapons get there? This is one question that could be asked and one of the things that will be known in full detail one day when some documents are declassified, because the day will come when absolutely everything will be known.

One could also ask where those seven nuclear weapons are because their manufacturers say they have been destroyed. That is all that those of the apartheid regime would say. The ANC leaders do not know. Nobody has answered that question. But, again, there are still a lot of questions that have never been answered.

Who supported Mobutu [Sese Seko]? The United States and Europe did. Where are the billions that Mobutu took from the Congo? Which bank is keeping them? Who protected and looked after him or inherited his immense fortune?

I could go on offering many similar examples. Who supported the acts of aggression against the Arab countries? The United States did.

I am in absolutely no way an anti-Semite, far from it. But, we have been very critical of the wars against the Arab countries, the massive evictions, the diaspora of Palestinians and other Arabs. Who supported those wars? And there are many other overt or covert wars and other similar incidents that I am not going to mention which have been done and continue to be done by those who want to sweep away sovereignty or the principles of sovereignty, in the name of humanitarian reasons. Of course, that is only one of the pretexts but not the only one as we see in Africa.

The Africans themselves are rightly concerned about tackling the problems of peace in their continent. They are trying to unite. They have a strong sense of unity. They also have their regional groupings and are trying to settle their conflicts. But who occupied and exploited Africa for centuries? Who kept it in poverty and underdevelopment? Who drew those border lines that cut through ethnic groups now separated by them? With great wisdom, really great wisdom, the Africans, from the time they started emerging as independent states, set out the principle of the inviolability of the frontiers whereby the inherited borders were sacred. Otherwise, a huge number of conflicts would have unleashed in Africa.

The colonial powers created all that. They are responsible for centuries of exploitation, backwardness and poverty. Are we going to resort to a racist interpretation of the reasons for the poverty of those African peoples when it is a known fact that, in that continent, various civilizations had attained remarkable progress at a time when in Berlin, Paris and many other places of civilized Europe there were only wandering tribes? A thousand years before, there already existed a civilization in Egypt, Ethiopia and other parts of Africa.

The United States emerged as a nation only twenty centuries later. What is the cause of that poverty if not the colonialist, slavery, neo-colonialist, capitalist and imperialist system that reigned in the world in the past centuries? Why could those peoples not benefit from the fruits of science and human progress? Those who exploited them for centuries are guilty for this.

At one time, they also had China semi-colonized and humiliated. It is common knowledge that, in the past century, they used cannon shots to open up Japan's ports to world trade. It is a known fact that the British empire sent its troops to conquer a portion of Chinese territory and, in a coalition with other European powers and the United States, it sent troops as far as Beijing. Thus came the invasions and wars to sell opium.

Now they want to invade countries where poppies are planted, and not by the country but by a number of hungry and sometimes desperate people. Impoverished nations, aware of the huge market for drugs in the United States – one which was not created by a Latin American country or any other nation in the world – plant poppies or coca for the colossal consumption of the industrialized and rich countries.

The question could be asked of how much drug per capita is consumed in the United States of America and in Europe. Possibly much more than in Brazil or Argentina, Uruguay or Paraguay, Central America or Mexico, or even in Colombia itself. The market is up North. It was a disgrace for our countries, those where the crop arose, that there was such a high demand in the United States.

the great promoter, the great patron, the great fatherly educator

This is important because yesterday was hardly the first time that they publicly tried to promote the doctrine that they have been elaborating against sovereignty, that they have been discussing among themselves and with other NATO members, the one they have been advancing little by little, step by step.

The so-called global threats are also considered enough reason to fully justify an intervention. We will quote three of those threats: drugs, terrorism and the possession of weapons of mass destruction. Of course, this has nothing to do with them. They can have all the weapons of mass destruction they want, thousands of nuclear weapons, as it is the case of the United States. They can also have rockets that, with great accuracy, they can position anywhere in the world and a whole arsenal of laboratories devoted to producing biological weapons – they have used biological weapons against us – and any other kind of weapons. They have reached agreements among themselves to eliminate chemical and biological weapons. But, at the same time, they develop other even more deadly weapons.

According to the doctrine described, a Third World country could have a nuclear weapon and, for that reason, become the target of a sudden air strike and invasion. And, what about all those who possess nuclear weapons? It is a matter of wars, either pre-emptive or punitive, to preserve the monopoly of nuclear weapons and other kinds of weapons of mass destruction which are very far from being humanitarian.

The fourth reason is the massive violation of human rights.

Up to now, the great promoter, the great patron, the great fatherly educator and supporter of those who committed massive violations of human rights has been the United States of America. Massive destruction of the infrastructure and economy of a country, as it has just happened in Serbia; genocide using bombs to deprive millions of people of crucial services and their means of life; genocidal wars like the one launched against Vietnam. They were the culprits.

I am not talking of the time when more than half of Mexico was conquered. I am not talking of Hiroshima and Nagasaki, a terrorist experiment into the effects of nuclear weapons on cities where hundreds of thousands of people lived. I am talking about things that have happened since World War II. Who were their allies? Why did the Franco government in Spain remain in power for almost 30 years after the end of a world war against fascism that lasted six vicious years and cost no less than 50 million lives? Because he had the support of the United States which wanted to have military bases there. Who supported utterly repressive governments in countries like Korea? They did. Who really supported the massive carnage of ethnic groups like Chinese, for example, or of communists or left-wing people in Indonesia? They did. Who supported the horrendous apartheid regime? They did.

There has been no bloody and repressive government, no massive violator of human rights that has not been their ally and has not been supported by them. In the case of Duvalier – to give you an example closer to home – who supported him? They did, until one day when they intervened in Haiti to overthrow him, for humanitarian reasons.

Do you realize what I mean? It is the development of a whole philosophy aimed at sweeping away the United Nations Charter and the principles of national sovereignty. The doctrine can be divided into three categories of intervention: humanitarian interventions due to internal conflicts; interventions due to global threats, which we have already described, and interventions due to external conflicts, to which are added the very confusing Yankee concept of 'diplomacy supported by force'. This means, for example, that if Colombia cannot solve its internal conflict – a difficult battle, of course – if it cannot achieve peace, for which many are working, including Cuba, this could become a reason for intervention. At the same rate, if it does not succeed in eradicating drug cultivation it could be the target of an armed intervention.

I have tried to collect precise information on what is happening with drugs in Colombia, how encompassing the phenomenon is and how many hectares of drug are planted. Some have told me that there are about 80,000 hectares of coca, just coca. It has been growing. And some have talked to me about up to a million people working in the cultivation of coca and the harvesting of leaves.

I asked about coffee and they told me that there are problems because the salary of a coffee harvester can come to 10 or 12 US dollars while those who harvest the coca leaves or clean the plantations, weed the crop and do other similar activities, earn five or six times higher wages.

What I do not know yet is whether they fertilize it although that is, seemingly, a natural process. Perhaps, with a certain regime of rain and climate the coca plant fertilizes itself. Maybe it is like the *marabú*. The *marabú* is a very harmful plant for agriculture here, terribly aggressive and thorny. It reproduces and spreads easily. It cannot be used to feed the animals but it is a leguminous plant, so it does not need to be fertilized. It feeds itself from nitrogen through the nodular bacteria in its roots. Apparently, something similar happens with the coca.

Can you imagine what the situation must be like in a country where a million people in the rural areas can earn 50, 60, 70 US dollars in the coca fields while the same working day in other crops would bring them 10 US dollars at most? And, at harvest time – and coca can be harvested three times a year – it is only a matter of pulling off leaves.

Trying to learn about this I have almost become an expert by now, just by asking questions. I say: 'Tell me, explain to me, are they all small plantations?' They tell me: 'No, there are large estates of hundreds of hectares and plantations of as much as thousands of hectares'. I ask: 'How much, for example, does somebody with a hectare of coca earn?' 'That one receives the least,' they say. The others receive more: the ones who turn it into the basic paste, the other ones who refine it and, fundamentally, those who market it. Before that phase, many airlines, transport companies and firms providing other services obtain high incomes. When such a cancer is introduced in a society it becomes a real tragedy, in every sense, because the danger that internal consumption may spread is multiplied. We are striving against it ourselves. You were saying that tourism should not affect culture or damage the national identity but it can sometimes damage health, if prostitution, for instance, is promoted.

When I talked to you about the US dollar, I told you that it circulates here. The measures that we have had to take made its circulation necessary. Well, but that dollar neither escapes the country nor becomes volatile. It is a dollar that circulates here whose value decreases every day. It has to do with a historical stage. At the moment, we are not so interested in lowering its value, rather, depending on the resources available, we are interested in raising wages in Cuban pesos, without letting the peso lose its current parity in US dollars.

It is good not to be a part of the International Monetary Fund! The truth is that the circulation of the US dollar, coupled with the unrestricted entry and exit of a lot of visitors, can encourage the drugs trade and the cultivation of drugs which forces us to be very watchful.

To get back to the problem of Colombia, somebody told me: 'One hectare of coca can provide an income of up to 4,000 US dollars.' I said: 'And if it were planted with corn, in that tropical and rainy plain?' You all know that the Colombian plains are not corn-growing area. The corn-growing area is a bit further North, at the same height as the central plains in the United States and also at the height of Europe, although corn originated in this hemisphere, in Mexico, Central and South America. Therefore, I assure you that planting corn there without fertilizers or anything would hardly give the peasant one ton per hectare. A ton of corn on the international market is worth more or less between 100 and 150 US dollars. In Argentina and other places, the export price has decreased to 90 US dollars. We have to import them, so we know the cost of each of these grains.

I have not talked about wheat, which cannot be planted there. Corn, for example, can be planted for self-consumption or to market it. How much is the producer paid for his ton of corn that the middleman then sells in the market? On the other hand, if custom barriers are also removed, then the grains produced abroad would enter freely. That is what the United States wants from its trade agreements with Latin America.

In that case, the Colombian would eat American corn because it is produced cheaper than Colombian corn. They obtain six, seven or more tons and cultivation there is very mechanized. They produce it cheaper than the French. The French should be careful about American corn because they will put it in France at a lower price than it costs to produce a ton of corn there. That is why agricultural issues become the great obstacle for the free-trade agreements.

The Yankees are reckoning: 'I will give you some industrial advantages as soon as possible. I will give you an X number of years for you to start reducing the tariffs on the grains that I will export until the day that entry is unrestricted.' We know very well what is going to happen: these countries will end up with no corn farming, then corn will be very expensive and to the extent that the price rises there will not be any other corn but the American's.

But, how much would our farmer earn after changing a hectare of coca for one of corn? Instead of 4,000 US dollars, he would earn whatever he is paid for his corn by a middleman or by a chain of middlemen. It might be 60 or 100 US dollars. So, where are the possibilities for alternative crops?

They have already created a drug culture. They have alienated millions of people with their voracious market and their money-laundering. It has been the United States banks that have laundered the vast majority of the funds coming from drugs. They are not just a market but practically the financiers, the drug money launders. Moreover, they do not want to spend money to really eradicate the growing of coca or poppies, although they invest billions in repressive procedures.

I think that, theoretically, there might be a solution but it would cost billions of US dollars, even if those resources were rationally invested. What are they going to do with the men who live massively on drug growing? Are they going to be exterminated? They could also go there themselves and invade that country on account of 'a global threat' even if the drug problem cannot be controlled with simple repressive measures. Of course, invading it would be madness because, the heat in the forests of the Colombian plains would finish off their soldiers used to drinking Coca-Cola on combat missions, cold water at every hour, ice cream of the best quality. Actually, Vietnam is a well-known case in point and they get more and more used to every kind of luxury and comfort.

The mosquitoes and the heat would almost suffice to finish them off but they could cause a real disaster if they intervened there to eradicate drugs. Certainly, that would not be the kind of war to use B-2 bombers because the coca crops cannot be fought with laser-guided bombs, smart missiles or planes. There, they would surely have to go in with ground forces, either to wipe out an irregular force in the jungle or to eradicate crops. On the other hand, since they describe guerrilla warfare as terrorism, insurgency and a great risk – practically a global threat – there we have a country with two possible pretexts for intervention. I am talking of two categories: internal conflicts and drugs. Two causes for intervention according to the theories they are trying to impose.

Would an invasion or the bombing of Colombia solve the internal conflict? I wonder if NATO could solve that problem now that it is establishing the right of action beyond its borders. In principle, they agreed on that during the 50th anniversary celebration. Along such lines you can imagine so many cases. Is there anybody who believes that could be the solution?

I know, through opinion polls, that in their desperation at the violence and the problems in the country, not a few people in Colombia itself – actually a number of people worth taking into consideration – have expressed support for the idea that, if there is no other solution to the violence, it be resolved through the intervention of an outside force.

Of course, the fighting and patriotic tradition of the Colombian people should not be overlooked. I am sure that such an act of madness against a country like Colombia, in the style of what they did in Serbia, would be a disaster, absolute madness. But, no one knows, really, since international law, the principles of respect for sovereignty and the United Nations Charter no longer provide a reliable coverage and that could be a decision taken on their own by a Mafia armed to the teeth, which is what NATO has become.

The rest of the countries, ours included, cannot feel safe. Not at all! And there is the risk of insane actions that cost millions of lives. I am sure that an invasion of Colombia, that is, the implementation of this doctrine in Colombia would cause millions of deaths. That is a country where violence is rampant, where 30,000 people meet a violent death every year – a figure that is well above the average of violent deaths in the rest of Latin America.

Now, would an invasion by NATO forces solve the problem? No, but then, they would say as Solana did: 'Diplomatic or peaceful ways were exhausted.'

As Latin Americans, we should try to cooperate with Colombia, with the country itself, to help it achieve a fair peace, one that would benefit everybody.

There are formulas that, in my view, are so complex and difficult that I would tend to call them utopian because there is not one war there, but three or four. There are significant guerilla forces with political motivations but divided into two organizations fighting on their own. There are extremely repressive paramilitary forces at the service of the landowners and there are the forces of the drug growers, people armed to shoot down the crop-spraying helicopters, for example.

Colombia's situation is really complex. I have mentioned it in the context of the theories that I have described and the consequences that they might have.

just once is enough, is it not?

We should all help! It should never be said that the diplomatic and peaceful ways have been exhausted, the discussions should never stop. A process has already begun. Venezuela wants to cooperate. We cooperate to the extent of our possibilities and so do other countries. Colombia's domestic problems have no solution other than a political and peaceful settlement. This is crystal clear to me. Let us help the Latin Americans find these solutions!

If one day we had a federation of Latin American states, if there were unity, we would give up many of the attributes of our sovereignty. Then, domestic order would become the prerogative of a supranational state that is ours and does not belong to a foreign superpower that has nothing to do with us or to a powerful Europe.

We want to involve in friendly relations with Europe, also in trade, science and technological development, but it also has absolutely nothing to do with the domestic problems of our countries. We would surely be capable of solving our domestic problems ourselves politically, without bombings, destruction and bloodshed. We do not need anyone to do it for us.

Why are they going to demolish the principles of the United Nations? I could begin by exploring some examples. It would occur to me to ask how the NATO doctrine would apply to Russia, for example, if a conflict broke out there like the one in Chechnya or various other conflicts that might arise from the fact that the state is made up of numerous different ethnic groups that also have different religious beliefs. Also, an internal conflict might arise among the Slav Russians themselves because some are communists and others are liberals or neo-liberals or some position in between. And then what? Would they invade Russia? Would they unleash a nuclear war?

Russia was a superpower. There used to be two superpowers. Today, there is one superpower and one power. What difference does it make? That the power can destroy the superpower three or four times over and the superpower can destroy the power 12 or 14 times over. In other words, quite a few more times over. But just once is enough, is it not? Can they go about applying such theories?

At the UN Security Council they have had intensive discussions. A draft resolution has been passed by that body. If you would bear with me, really, I could tell you some even more interesting things. But I want to finish with this, I mean, the matter of the doctrines that are being developed. That is why I asked the previous question.

I will ask another: if there is a conflict in India, it might be a border conflict – right now, there is artillery fire on the Indo–Pakistani border – can the doctrine be applied there? Would it apply where there are more than a 100 million Pakistanis and, on the other side, almost a billion Indians, from many different ethnic groups? Can such a deranged theory be applied in countries that, furthermore, possess nuclear weapons? I do not know whether they have 50, 100 or 20 nuclear weapons. But just 20 would be a huge amount and the war could become nuclear. How many would die enforcing this American formula inexplicably supported by Europe? Total madness!

I will go a bit further: What if the conflict is in China, where there are different ethnic groups, in a country with a population of more than 1,250 million and with an extraordinary war experience, courage, fighting spirit. This is the case with every people, of course, but the Chinese were forced to confront many acts of aggression and difficulties.

We also remember that during the Korean War as [General]

MacArthur's troops were approaching the Chinese border and some were already talking about attacking the other side, a million Chinese combatants crossed the border and reached the present demarcation line. One million! Of course, the number of fatal casualties could have been – I cannot guarantee the exact number – perhaps up to 200,000 Chinese soldiers. The United States already had all sorts of bombers and other weapons but the human masses could not be contained and they would not have been able to achieve victory, not even with nuclear weapons.

How would the doctrine apply in China, a country they are constantly harassing with campaigns about human rights as they do with our own country? There have been some significant problems there widely exploited by Western propaganda. But, imagine how confused those young people were who took as a symbol the Statue of Liberty, as it stands at the entrance of the port of New York. They must have been widely alienated to choose what has become a symbol tainted by the hypocrisy and voracity of an empire that goes around suffocating and insulting every idea of justice and true human freedom.

It is striking that this happened in a country with a culture thousands of years old and a much more solid identity than that of any of us, that is, a more integrated country, more distant from the West in terms of language, culture, traditions and many other things. It is not a country like ours, which has a lot of ingredients from Western customs and culture, but a country that has often been humiliated and where an extraordinary social revolution eradicated age-old famines. It is a country that, in barely 50 years, raised to its current prestige and the impressive place it occupies in the world.

How would they solve it? If they feel like it, the imperialists and their allies could declare any incident that occurs in areas of China that have been turned into bones of contention a massive violation of human rights. Buddhist Tibet, for instance, is mentioned and certain Muslim minorities in the north-west. We closely follow, through the international press dispatches, China's constant harassment by the West. Any domestic political problem could be considered a massive violation of human rights. They constantly go to great lengths to provoke it, moved by petty propaganda purposes and the stupid attempt to do with China what they did with the USSR. They simply fear that great nation.

Of course, the Chinese are wise politicians – that is why people talk about the Chinese wisdom – and they do not easily make the mistakes that a team of serious and skilled leaders should not make. They would not invade a country to take it over. They are, indeed, very zealous in matters relating to their own affairs. They strictly follow the principle of non-interference in the internal affairs of other countries. For many years, they have been demanding the return of Taiwan to Chinese territory but they are ready to wait peacefully for a hundred years. Their mindset is that of a millennia-old patience, so they talk about what they intend to do in the next 50 or 100 years as if it were tomorrow or the day after.

Any of these problems might be an excuse to send B-2 bombers, all sorts of missiles and laser-guided bombs. Some of the principles of their absurd and arrogant doctrine could serve as an excuse to attack China. Is that not an insane proposition? I am no longer talking about Colombia, I am talking about China. I am talking about Russia or India or the conflict between India and Pakistan. We will see if those in NATO and their Marshall – their leader or Marshall Secretary-General – are really excited enough to solve the conflict in Kashmir with a 'humanitarian intervention'.

I ask: what is that doctrine for? Why think about such methods? Whom are they going to apply them to? Only to smaller countries that have no nuclear weapons and to the rest of the world, wherever there might be a problem among the many that constantly arise.

we, Cuban revolutionaries, can say: 'and if we die, what is life?'

Such formulas do not apply to us, just in case anyone thinks that we are concerned by what might happen to us. Putting aside all conceit or boastfulness, our country, which has endured such hard trials, can sing *The Pirate's Song*.

> And if I die
> What is life?
> I already gave it up
> when the slave yoke I shook off
> as any brave man ought.

I still remember some of those lines which were in *The Hundred*

Best Poems in Spanish Language. Nowadays, you do not see such books around much, but at a certain time, when we did not have many works of literature, I took to learning such poems almost by heart and I still remember some of them.

We, Cuban revolutionaries, can say: 'And if we die, what is life?' and there are a lot of us, Cuban revolutionaries. We know that no true revolutionary, no true leader of the Cuban revolution would hesitate to die if our country became the target of an aggression.

I will say more, because we deeply analyse all their technology and their tactics and there is no war, big or small, and no criminal and cowardly bombing that we have not studied well. Aside from the fact that it will not be easy for them to find an excuse.

They are always inciting and scheming against Cuba, trying to stir up conflicts inside our country. They go to great lengths to create any kind of internal conflict that would justify monstrous crimes like they have just committed against the Serbs.

Those irresponsible people who in our country put themselves at the service of the United States and receive a salary from the US Interests Section are really toying with sacred things. They are toying with the lives of our people and they should be aware of that. The empire, knowing that Cuba would not give in, longs to accumulate enough forces with its blockade, its propaganda and its money to create internal conflicts. We are not talking of family remittances, we are talking of the United States government money. It has been publicly recognized there as well as in its own laws or amendments. They have recently declared that any American can send money to any Cuban. They have practically said: 'Let each American buy a Cuban.' And I said to myself: 'We should raise the price since there is one Cuban to 27 Americans.'

They authorize family remittances, but no more than 300 US dollars every three months. Cuba is the only country in the world with such restrictions. No, they do not raise by a dime the amount authorized for people of Cuban descent to sent remittances to their relatives but they invite Americans to send remittances to any Cuban. Perhaps, they will work through the telephone book, I do not know. They also give money to whatever small group or faction, to anyone. In their eagerness to stir up conflict, they have so declared and they have passed legislation about sending money. It is a serious matter. Extremely serious!

In their arrogance and disdain, they do not accept that Cuba is resisting. It is so hard for them to accept that they would like to vanish us from Earth, like they tried to do with Serbia. It is just that here it is different, or rather not. I would absolutely not question the Serbs' heroism and courage. Absolutely not. A country is not braver than any other, what makes people brave are their convictions and certain moral values. It can sometimes be religious conviction that leads a person to martyrdom, or it can be a political conviction served with religious fervor.

For example, our doctors who are in very isolated places in some countries of this continent or in neighbouring Haiti show a heroic attitude, the morality of missionaries, like true priests working for human health, pastors at the service of life, of values. I was reading today that some journalists had left for Haiti in order to inform the people and the relatives of those stationed there on the work that they are doing in the remotest places. Many of those doctors are women, some with children here, and they work in faraway places which can sometimes only be reached after three days of walking through swampy ground.

Some people have been contesting or rather trying to create unrest about our doctors in one of those fraternal countries. They are disputing our doctors' degrees. Ah!, but as soon as they ask, we will humbly and immediately forward them the curriculum vitae of each of those doctors and the grades they obtained in school, at the university, the specialist courses they have done, the surgeries they have performed, the lives they have saved. It would be wonderful to send the records of every one of them!

Our doctors are working there with humility and dedication in compliance with agreements signed by the governments. They are not there as an imposition. The moment any government tells us that their presence is inconvenient or that it creates any political problems, we shall immediately withdraw our doctors. This is it. But they work as missionaries, it could be said like true heroes. We know this very well because we are informed of what they are doing and we talk at great length with some of the people in charge of their activity when they come here. Our doctors' work is the expression of their own values.

We can say with satisfaction that if the World Health Organization wanted to implement a health programme, or Europe, even our neighbours up north if they wanted to salve their consciences a little and were ready to contribute with the medicines, we would be able to send 10,000 doctors wherever they are needed in Latin America. We also have doctors in the north of Sub-Saharan Africa, working there for free in an ambitious health programme.

If this country – I have to say it again – if we sent one out of every three doctors on such missions, the two remaining would carry out their work and health care in our country would not be hurt. And, if we sent one out of every three we would still be the country with the highest rate of doctors per capita among all countries in the world – higher than industrial Europe, higher than Sweden, higher than Denmark and, of course, higher than the United States, Canada and other great industrialized nations. Yes, a poor and blockaded country can also do things. This is a fact. And we have more teachers, too, and possibly more art instructors per capita than any of those countries.

I state the same thing about sports because we have about 30,000 qualified physical education and sports teachers, most of whom are university graduates. They know not only how to palpate a muscle but they know what muscle it is that they are palpating because they have a university education.

We also have another small merit, which is the highest number of gold medals per capita in the Olympic Games. And we shall continue to have them, even if the games go professional because we have just proven that our modest amateur sport can compete with good professional teams. It is obvious that a small and poor country can do things. They are wrong to underestimate us.

Really, this is not bragging; on the contrary, we prefer to discuss our mistakes, to criticize ourselves but after seeing the insolence, the demagogy, the lies and the slanders against Cuba, we have no other choice but to talk about some of the things we have done. Anything else would be foolish, I mean, boasting here about what we have done. We are rather very critical of ourselves for not having done more and for not having done it better. That is how it is. I am saying it in all honesty. I think that one of the reasons for the resistance and the survival of the revolution is that the leaders here are never complacent. We hope and we dream that they will continue the same way in the future as well. And, of course, we have great confidence in our people.

I was telling you that if it occurred to them to carry out one of those mad actions against us, they would not only find the people I have described but one with a sound political culture and important, sacred values to defend. This fight has been going on for many years and I can tell you that we will not ask for a truce. No truce! The people in charge of this Revolution would die rather than make a single concession of principles to the empire.

honour is not negotiable!

Rather than relinquishing a single atom of our sovereignty, those of us responsible for leading our people in peace and in war, in every endeavour, we would not survive capitulation. We are deeply committed to what we have done all our lives and because we feel it very intensively, because our commitment rests on convictions and values, we would stand right under the bombs rather than surrender.

In such an adventure it is not difficult to die. There is no greater glory! At least, we would be setting an example for others! The Yugoslavian people set an example. They resisted the most unbelievable bombings for almost 80 days, without hesitation. We knew about the spirit of the people there through our diplomatic representatives.

I do not intend to criticize anybody. I respect the decision that any government might take and it does not escape me that decisions are difficult under certain circumstances. But, for us they will not be at all difficult because we solved that problem a long time ago. If they were to do that here, they would be defeated, as simple as that. Not even a genocide would give them victory because there is a limit to their killing capacity, and I firmly believe that, if the aggressors had had to extend those bombings for 15 or 20 more days, the world and the European public opinion would not have accepted it. A few days before the famous peace formula was imposed on Yugoslavia, the world opinion was increasingly turning against the aggressors. I have a large number of newspaper articles reflecting exactly that.

Of course, nobody would have been able to impose that on us because we have been here alone, all by ourselves, all alone for a long while, near the mightiest power that ever existed. So, who could come here to impose it on us?

Nobody could. And we do not need any mediator. Honour is not negotiable! Our homeland is not negotiable! Dignity is not negotiable! Independence, sovereignty, history and glory are not negotiable!

There would be no negotiating with us for a cessation of bombings. I will advance that if they started bombing some day, they would have to continue for a hundred years if it was a war from the air they wanted to make; or they would have to stop dropping bombs because as long as there were a few combatants still alive in this country, they would be forced to send ground troops. I would like to know what would happen if they did that.

As I was saying, we do not do anything foolish that they can use as an excuse. Your can see how patient we have been with that (Guantanamo) base. It is a small piece of Cuban land and we have every right to have it back. The people here have had quite a radical view of the issue. Not us, we are patient. We say: 'No, it is much more important to liberate the world than to liberate that beloved piece of land that we will never give up.' They would have loved it if we had started a strong national movement claiming the base in order to have an easy pretext for their adventures, to deceive US and world public opinion, to say that we have attacked them. Before concluding, I will show you some things in this respect. But they have never had the remotest chance of saying that Cuba has been hostile or aggressive toward the American military personnel stationed there.

What can they say about us on humanitarian issues? That we have not a single illiterate, that we have not a single child without a school, not a single person without medical care. That there are no beggars here although there are sometimes irresponsible families who send out their children on errands. That is associated with tourism and it affects, if not our identity, at least our honour. There is nobody abandoned in the streets.

What can they say? That we have a massive number of excellent doctors as I have been telling you about. What else can they say? That we can save hundreds of thousands of lives each year in our hemisphere and in Africa.

What did we tell the Haitians? That we are willing to put forward a plan to save some 30,000 lives a year, 25,000 of them children's lives.

What was our proposal to the Central Americans? A plan to save, every year, as many lives as the hurricane took, if it actually took 30,000. That figure decreased later because many that were missing began to show up. As we said, the lives that could be saved every year could be as many as those taken by the hurricane, if the highest figure announced was true – and that is a conservative estimate. The truth is that, on that programme, we were ready to contribute the required staff and we asked that any industrial country, no matter which, contribute the drugs. Why is it that all those spending so many billions on bombs and genocide do not use a little money to save lives?

I told you the other day about how they attributed loathsome things to us and I mentioned a number of them. I told you and I will repeat it now: not a single person is tortured in this country! Not a single political assassination! Not a single vanished person! Forty years have already passed since the triumph of the Revolution despite all the conspiracies and all the efforts made to divide us, to subvert the Revolution. They have crashed against our people's iron-like unity and patriotism, against their political culture. All this under extremely difficult circumstances.

I am absolutely certain that very few people would resist the almost 10 years that we have resisted after loosing all our markets and supply sources and with a tightened blockade. They underestimated us.

Also, if they carried out one of the acts of madness mentioned, they would be underestimating us and I do not think they underestimate us quite that much, I really do not. I will say no more. We are not defending ourselves here but the right of other peoples who do not have our possibilities or our unity or the fighting capacity that we have as an organized and prepared people.

I already told you, and I am not dramatizing, that we have no need for that kind of new specialist who emerged from this war in Yugoslavia with the category of mediator. They can come only to report that they will proceed to suspend the bombings or withdraw troops or to cease all hostilities. This much we dare say: no weapon has been invented that can conquer man! We are not afraid of those repulsive and cowardly wars where they do not risk a single life! They are nauseating, disgusting but they only make us better socialists and better revolutionaries. That is all.

it was disintegration time!

I was telling you that an important battle was fought at the United Nations. Here is the famous Resolution. They are incorrigible cheats, mediocre and incompetent politicians. I brought some papers but I will just use a few things I underlined.

Well, this is the agreement that was passed, the draft Resolution. Who sponsored it? Germany, a NATO country; Canada, a NATO country; the United States, a leading country and chief of NATO; the Russians are among the sponsors because they reached previous agreements in the Group of Eight but they made a critical speech there; France, a NATO country; Italy, a NATO country; the Netherlands, a NATO country; the United Kingdom of Great Britain and Northern Ireland, a NATO country. I counted them and I saw that there were seven NATO countries among the 12 sponsors of the draft in the Security Council – seven countries involved in the aggression.

There was also, Gabon, a French neocolonial dominion and Slovenia, a former Yugoslav republic. This was the first one that – heedless of the constitutional rules set forth when the Yugoslav Federation was created recognizing the right to secession and the procedures to accomplish it – encouraged by Germany and Austria unilaterally declared its Independence avoiding any legal formality. Yes, there had undoubtedly been previous groundwork. On the other hand, it was disintegration time!

One of the republics separated constitutionally through a plebiscite. That was Macedonia, but Slovenia declared its Independence on June 25, 1991. In Europe, there were doubts over what to do. Later on came Croatia's declaration of independence, that is, two splits avoiding all constitutional procedures. And this, as our ambassador to the United Nations said, was promoted by some European countries and later unanimously supported by the West.

This is important because when that country emerged – the heroic Yugoslavia that kept even Hitler's troops at bay – the Socialist Federal Republic of Yugoslavia lived in peace despite centuries-old national, ethnic, cultural and religious struggles. That area of Yugoslavia, between the Ottoman Empire and the Austro-Hungarian Empire, was a battlefield. It is a well known story that the Ottomans reached the outskirts of Vienna.

We have been reading a lot of background information and, really, there were people who contributed to the so-called ethnic wars that broke out in the 1990s, people who helped, certainly not on purpose since I do not attribute it to a premeditated and cynical concept but to irresponsible acts. Anyway, they unleashed the disintegration of Yugoslavia and it all began, as I said, with Slovenia on June 25, 1991 when avoiding any legal procedure Slovenia declared its Independence and its leaders took command of the troops corresponding to that republic, since every republic had its self-defense troops; they were about 40,000 men. As I understand it, some 2,000 young draftees from the neighboring Croatian republic left for Slovenia. There was practically no combat. There were only such pressures.

The disease began to spread. Another republic, Croatia, did the same. In that case, more violent conflicts broke out.

What happened? These republics could very well have followed the constitutional procedures. Yugolsavia was no longer a socialist country. It was a country that had established all the capitalist and market standards. It was not the old Yugoslavia of [Marshal] Tito and of a later period. It was a capitalist country with the multi-party system officially recommended by the West.

A very influential factor was that in 1981, ten years before this happened, Slovenia's GDP was five times the per capital GDP of the rest of Yugoslavia. They began to feel that the poorer republics were a burden and they were encouraged to move toward closer economic integration with the West. Some supported them – as I said – some gave them weapons at that stage, even before they had declared independent. One of their leaders has admitted this much.

On June 21, 1996, in a programme on the Ljublijana television specially devoted to the fifth anniversary of Independence, President Kucan conceded that 'Slovenia was already building up its army before 1990 in anticipation of a war.' In the same interview, the Slovene president added: 'The European Union played a great role in making possible the breakup from Yugoslavia.'

This is real history. I do not want to offend anybody nor do I mean to hurt anyone. I abide by the facts, the historical facts that we have been looking at again together with some information we already had when this conflict broke out.

It was irresponsible and truly criminal to encourage and support the disintegration of that country which had achieved the miracle of living in peace for 45 years.

There were different factors bearing on the situation there, both economic and of a nationalist character, and there were a lot of people in Europe who understood the potential consequences. I have spoken with European leaders, European politicians who understood that this was very risky. However, one day two countries, specifically Germany and Austria, officially recognized Slovenia and Croatia and, immediately, the rest of Europe followed, thus beginning all sorts of conflicts that we now know about.

There were difficulties in Kosovo where there was a strong nationalist movement. The Albanian Kosovars or Kosovar Albanians were already a large majority. I remember that even when [Marshal] Tito was alive, many Serbs had migrated to Serbia because they felt unsafe. In 1974, the Constitution was amended and Kosovo was granted autonomy – I have not read that Constitution – but that is precisely the Serbs' birthplace. There are many historical sites there that they value highly. Some of those sites have suffered with the bombings. But I do not know whether that Constitution – that I am trying to obtain – which granted autonomy to the Kosovo province, gave it the right to secession, as it did with the republics. Anyway, it was not declared a republic but an autonomous province. I assume that it did not have that right recognized and that, in any case, there would have been a process, like in Macedonia.

What began in 1991 has continued until today and nobody knows when it will end. There were all sorts of wars and blood was unquestionably shed from both sides. That is the truth, as I see it.

Now then, instead of starting to supposedly straighten out those countries, it would have been better if they had not been disrupted, if they had not been disorganized. Of course, living standards were largely different in Macedonia and Slovenia, very different. There was a Constitution by virtue of which the Socialist Federal Republic was established. It had the word 'socialist' before but more or less after the perestroika it was removed, that much is clear. Its present name is Federal Republic of Yugoslavia. That is, the name of what is left because what remained was Serbia and Montenegro since Kosovo was not a republic. What is left is called the Federal Republic of Yugoslavia, is it not? I have some papers here but I will not be looking for the exact name. We even have here the UN Security

Council resolution: 'Federal Republic of Yugoslavia,' that's it. The word 'socialist' was removed long ago.

The government may call itself socialist because you know that there are many governments where there are socialist parties but the countries are not socialist. There are socialist parties in many places and in the government, but this does not mean that the country is socialist or that it plans to be so. They are countries with free enterprise, neo-liberalization, pure capitalism.

As for Yugoslavia, our position is based on principles, both with respect to Serbs and with respect to Kosovars. We defend their right to autonomy. Moreover, we defend not only their right to have their own culture, their religious beliefs, their national rights and feelings but also if one day the Kosovars of all ethnic groups and the rest of Serbia decided to separate peacefully and democratically, once an equitable and just peace had been achieved and not one imposed from outside by means of war, we would support them.

No one knows what will happen with Montenegro. During the war Montenegro behaved the best it could for NATO's taste. It volunteered some criticisms, some opposition, and perhaps that is why its quota of bombs was much lower than Serbia's. I have read many messages sent by the aggressors to Montenegro encouraging it to secede and it was accorded special treatment during the war. All the bombs were for Serbia.

When the agreement reached by the Group of Eight refers to substantial autonomy for the Kosovars, one could ask: does it mean the kind of autonomy that Macedonia used to have? We do not know but, in that case, there would be a peaceful road to independence. There are many aspects on which Serbs and Kosovars can agree. It is beyond question that most of the Kosovo population are not Serbs. The Serbs constitute a minority and it is very likely that after this dreadful war Serb civilians will follow the Serb troops out. It is apparent. News have come that they were exhuming their dead because it is part of their traditions to migrate with the remains of their ancestors.

I do not know what they will do. Messages are being sent discouraging a massive migration and violence against the Serbs living there. Those risks exist at the moment. Many are claiming victory but, who is accepting blame for all the factors that led to this situation and all the ethnic conflicts? A horrendous crime they are calling a victory. A victory they would have to be ashamed of because from the moral point of view if we are to talk about victory and defeat, the morally defeated were those who waged a cowardly war and dropped 23,000 bombs over Serbia, some of the most sophisticated, destructive and technologically advanced bombs. What a victory!

you either surrender or face extermination

Our UN ambassador estimated that the NATO countries' GDP is 1,013 times greater than Serbia's and that the Alliance member countries have 43 times more regular troops. But, regular troops are useless in an air war like it was waged there. The difference was zero to infinite. Bomber planes arriving from the United States were able to drop bombs from great distances without running the slightest risk. It was a war that lasted 80 days and in which 23,000 bombs were launched against a country while the aggressors did not have a single combat casualty. It was the first time in history that something like that happened.

It must be said that this war, of which nobody can be proud, is a cowadly war, the most cowardly of all wars ever waged. The alleged victory was morally Pyrrhic and the war a genocide.

Why was it a genocide? What is a genocide? The attempt to exterminate a population: you either surrender or face extermination. How long were the bombings going to last? They were talking of up to October or November but that was idle talk. We know very well how many European leaders felt. Many newspaper articles were published on the growing discontent and opposition to the bombings in Europe and even in the United States. And there was even greater opposition to ground troops involvement. In my view, NATO was in no condition to continue that bombing much longer. Neither Europe nor the world would have tolerated it. NATO would have broken apart if it had persisted on that path.

As I said that we had three comrades there with a cell phone, working day and night, round the clock, under the bombs and with the air-raid sirens, even when there was no electric power. We always asked them about the morale of the population, about the prevailing spirit. The people there covered the bridges with crowds; men, women and children went there so that they would not be destroyed. That was the case of the last bridge standing in Belgrade.

The NATO planes attacked all the bridges and there were times when it mostly attacked the electrical network. It destroyed virtually all the power plants leaving millions without light and energy. Imagine a house, if they had something to cook, how could they if there was no fuel, no light, no water? All those pumping systems operate with electricity. Take away the electricity and the cities are left without water. Destroy all the bridges and the cities are left without any supplies whatsoever.

When the electrical service, for example, is rendered useless a whole lot of basic services become useless too. Imagine intensive-care units without electricity or water; hospitals without electricity or water; schools without electricity or water; households, medical and educational facilities, all facilities and supplies cut off. So, it was not a war against the military, it was a war against the civilian population.

Then it occurred to Marshall Solana to make a solemn statement, that 'electric facilities were absolutely military objectives'. No one should be so arbitrary with words, ideas and concepts to justify a genocide. All means of life were under attack. The main workplaces were destroyed so half a million Serb workers were left jobless and it is not known how many more will be. Hospitals, schools, embassies, prisons, Kosovar convoys were attacked. They said that these had been failures.

I remember reading a dispatch about a General in the British air force who, after 15 or 20 days of bombing, said: 'Well, it is just that our pilots have been very restricted up to now. Now, each plane will simply go hunting a target.' They went hunting targets, whether it was a convoy of Kosovar refugees they attacked mistaken for Serb troops, or a prison where they killed 87 people; also, maternity and pediatric hospitals. There is a very long list of such incidents. Above all, admitting that a bomb might have been dropped by mistake, the destruction of all the bridges and electric systems could not be, and was not, a mistake.

What would have happened if the Serbs had continued resisting? How long could they have prolonged such barbaric actions?

The UN Security Council adopted a draft resolution. Of its 12 sponsors, seven belong to NATO, another is a neo-colony of one of the seven NATO co-sponsors and another one triggered the disintegration of Yugoslavia in 1991. There is also Japan, a member of the group of the seven richest countries – and this draft was by the Group of Seven – and the Russian Federation, which took part in the meeting of the Group of Seven plus Russia that agreed on a peace plan and sent its emissaries to Belgrade to submit it and Ukraine, a Slav country separated from Russia although it keeps normal relations with it and very good relations with NATO. These are the 12 sponsors of the draft resolution submitted to the UN Security Council and produced, in this case, by the Group of Eight.

What happened can be seen clearly, in strict chronological order.

Marshall Solana gave the order for the attack and the disciplined US Generals, who were leading the operation, began the attacks on the night of March 24. They were completely certain that the attacks would only last three days. Look at how senseless and shortsighted, irresponsible and poor calculators they were. They estimated that Serbia would immediately surrender after three days of bombings. The fourth day went by, then the fifth, the sixth, the seventh . . .

We have some interesting documents that might be published some day, various messages in different directions where our role as prophets shows, and the events unfolded exactly as we predicted on the basis of an elementary calculation of what was going to happen. We were familiar with the Yugoslavs' traditions: they fought against 40 of Hitler's divisions and among the countries that took part in that war it was Yugoslavia that had the highest percentage of dead compared to its total population. The Soviet Union had about 20 million, as was always said, with a population of about 250 million. Higher figures were given later but 20 million was the one always reported, a round figure. The Serbs must have had some 1,700,000 dead in that war. I cannot tell you right now how accurate that figure is but I do know that it was the country that suffered the highest number of dead with relation to its population. They fought then using methods of irregular warfare and a concept of fighting with the involvement of all the people.

Right now, the Serb troops are withdrawing from Kosovo with almost all their tanks, cannons and armoured vehicles. It is amazing! It is amazing that complete units are being withdrawn, as shown on television, despite the density and the intensity of the attacks launched against them. They were in perfect conditions for ground combat.

the people would surely have resisted indefinitely

I really believe that they should have developed other concepts. I say this in all sincerity. This is an issue to which we have given a lot of thought. They had complete units although this was not a war of conventional Serbian war units against NATO units. They could have used tanks, cannons and whatever they wanted but with the units organized in unconventional ways. Perhaps, or almost certainly, they had them deployed in a way that was absolutely appropriate for the type of war they might have had to wage. We have no information on what they did and how they did it.

We knew beforehand what was going to happen, namely, that they were going to resist. If it had not been for the pressures they came under from friends and enemies alike, which seems to have been enormous, possibly the Serb leaders would have continued to resist. I will say no more. The people would surely have resisted indefinitely. NATO would have had to decide on a ground campaign or else suspend the bombing and in a ground war it would not have been easy for NATO to overcome the growing political obstacles nor would the war ever have ended. That is my point of view.

Well then, the draft resolution by NATO and the Group of Eight was adopted and the bombings stopped. In one of its sections, the resolution adopted reads, and I quote, that the US Security Council 'Decides on the deployment in Kosovo, under United Nations auspices, of international civil and security presences,' the words seem so harmless, ' . . . and welcomes the agreement of the Federal Republic of Yugoslavia to such presences.' Well, it does not say what presences. International security forces, it does not say whose.

It later reads that it 'Requests the Secretary-General to appoint, in consultation with the Security Council, a Special Representative to control the implementation of the international civil presence.' The question is who is in command there? The United Nations leads the civil presence, 'and further requests the Secretary-General to instruct his Special Representative to coordinate closely with the international security presence to ensure that both presences operate towards the same goals and in a mutually supportive manner.'

It asks its man to coordinate with the leaders of those troops while still not saying which troops – a civil leadership which is the one under the orders of the United Nations – and it asks the civil representative to coordinate with the security forces, in case they pay any attention to him. It 'Authorizes Member States and relevant international organizations to establish the international security presence in Kosovo as set out in point 4 of annex 2 with all necessary means to fulfil its responsibilities under paragraph 9 below.' It *authorizes*, they are not under its command. It *invites*, knowing beforehand who were *invited*. It is said that many are called but few are chosen. It 'Affirms the need for the rapid early deployment of effective international civil and security presences to Kosovo, and demands,' a terribly strong word, 'that the parties cooperate fully in their deployment.' In other words, that the different countries cooperate fully. We are also ready to cooperate if they want doctors but not one soldier because that is not an internationalist or a peace mission. It is an imperialist mission with very specific objectives. We are ready to cooperate to save lives. As for the rest, the decisions taken by each one do not concern us.

It is known, however, that the British will have 13,000 troops in Kosovo – the main forces – with a British General in command. The number of Americans is unknown. Some marines have already landed in Greece – they will probably arrive in the thousands. The French too, and all the aggressors. The figure of Russians is not public although it is known more or less how many Russians are already there; a press dispatch has brought the news that somebody said that there could be between 2,000 and 10,000. Who is commanding them? We will see because this is a bone of contention.

As to the possibilities for the presence of Russian soldiers, a statement was made yesterday by the current Russian Prime Minister [Stepashin] which reads: 'The armed forces are in such a catastrophic state that the military-industrial complex and the army are barely surviving. We must remember this in next year's budget.' What will be next year's budget? Nobody knows. Even if it is catastrophic, they would have to cover the costs of the troops which will come to 4,000 or 5,000. If they get to 5,000, they would only be 10 per cent of the so-called security forces.

What is well known is that regardless of who accompanies NATO, it will be NATO that will have 90 per cent of the occupying troops under its direct command, and not only its own troops but also the accompanying

:roops. There will be countries, such as Ukraine, that will offer some
soldiers. A Latin American country might offer a small groups of soldiers,
some young draftees. But, NATO will have everything there in addition to
:he thousand planes that took part in the bombing.

The Russians will, at most, have a helicopter, a light aircraft to fly
from one place to another. The Ukrainians might have some jeeps and
maybe even a helicopter. NATO will have everything on air, land and sea
and command over everything. The discrepancy now is with the Russians
who are embittered, humiliated and threatened, that is the truth. Actually,
with that precedent anybody might think that any day now missiles, laser-
guided bombs and millions of other things could begin falling on them,
especially when it has been admitted that 'the armed forces are in a
catastrophic state', which does not exclude the fact that the strategic missiles
do work and they have thousands of them. Yes, they have thousands of
strategic missiles. They are a nuclear power and, of course, all that is
expensive.

The UN Security Council 'Welcomes the work in hand in the
European Union and other international organizations to develop a
comprehensive approach to the economic development and stabilization
of the region affected by the Kosovo crisis, including the implementation
of a Stability Pact for South Eastern Europe with broad international
participation in order to further the promotion of democracy, economic
prosperity, stability and regional cooperation.'

The adopted resolution does not say: the internaitonal
community should contribute to rebuilding everything there, whether
Kosovar or Serb. No, what the NATO leaders are declaring is that the
government that made an agreement with them, and yielded to the advice
or the pressures of the Group of Eight's mediators, must step down now
and appear before the International Tribunal for Yugoslavia where it has
been accused.

Not a word about building anything in Serbia. About
Montenegro, they do say that it will receive suitable treatment, that it has
behaved very well and accepted refugees. But, nothing about Serbia. Before,
they dropped bombs on them for having such a government and now, for
the same reason, they will not help them to feed themselves, and that after
all the destruction. Look how noble, how generous and humanitarian the
United States and NATO are! Do you not think? What is the fault of

children there aged from zero to one, ten, fifteen years old? What is the old people's fault? What is the fault of the pregnant women, the retired, ordinary men and women who have lived through such a traumatic experience?

Often, the most traumatizing about a bombing is the explosions, the noise. The Nazis, who have been quite well imitated in this merciless war – and I say this from my heart – used some terrifying sirens in their Stuka planes when dive-bombing their targets. I remember that war. I had just turned 13 when it began but I was interested in all the news and I read about it. I remember the war almost as if it were yesteday. In their combat planes, they had some sirens that made a hellish noise aimed at sowing fear, panic and disarray while they dropped their bombs, which were not at all like those of today. They were toy bombs compared to those dropped by NATO over Serbia.

The terror of bombings produces lifelong trauma, much more so in a child of three, four, five, six, seven, eight years, who remain day after day and every night under the noise of the sirens and the explosions. Would any doctor, any psychologist dare say that those children and millions of people will not endure a lifelong trauma with the terror they lived under for 80 days from the air-raid sirens plus the hellish roar of the combat planes engines as they flew at ground level, which is much more deafening than the Stuka sirens and with much more powerful explosions than those of the Nazi bombs?

Yet, they must now be punished: not one dime to rebuild a school of those they say were mistakenly destroyed, not one hospital, not one power plant. What are they going to live on? Well, now it is a hunger bombing. An agreement was signed with certain leaders who will handle things and they will know what they are doing. But, I consider it a crime to deny even a handful of wheat to the Serb people after dropping 23,000 bombs and missiles on them. Then, if the man presiding Serbia remains in government for three months or six or if he simply stays longer, a year – I do not know, nobody can foretell – the people will be subjected to a genocidal war for a year, all the civilians, all those who are in no way responsible for any ethnic cleansing or for the masses of refugees.

There were 20,000 refugees but when the massive bombings began people withdrew for many different reasons: out of fear or because they were afraid of being evicted or suppressed, or maybe because they were terrified by the bombings or afraid of dying. You can never say it is only one reason. What is the fault of the children, the civilians, the hundreds of thousands who were left jobless and other workers, the peasants, the farmers, the pensioners, the civilian population in general? What is their fault, really? It is a crime to keep them waiting until the government changes. To make them wait for a month is 30 times more criminal and a year would be 365 times more criminal. Each day that they are denied food is a crime.

I remember that during our liberation struggle we had an enemy force under siege, with no water or food because we had cut off their water supply and they had run out of food. Our combatants handed their cigarettes and their food to the exhausted soldiers who surrendered because a sense of chivalry had been created in the revolutionary troops and there was a policy in place for treating the enemy. If a policy like that does not exist, a war cannot be won. If you mistreat your enemies, if you torture them, they will never surrender. They will fight to their last bullet.

We had a strict policy in that sense: after 24 or 48 hours, they were set free. At the beginning, they fought very hard. Later, when they realized they were lost, they parleyed and the officers were allowed to leave with their pistols. We did not want to make them go hungry nor could we give them what little food we had. At times, we called in the International Red Cross, as we did during the last enemy offensive when we took hundreds of prisoners in two-and-a-half months of combat. During the war, we ended up with thousands of prisoners that we had taken in combat. Entire units were besieged and we treated them gently because they were our arm suppliers.

We did not receive arms from anybody during our short but intense liberation war while fighting against quite powerful forces but it did not occur to any of us to surrender. At a certain time I only had two rifles and other comrades were left with five. We were two armed groups when we met again, after a significant setback, to resume the struggle. Comrade Raul's group had five rifles and four men and my group had two rifles and three men. In total, we were seven men with seven rifles but we were not discouraged. Twenty-four months later, we attained victory.

This is not self-glorification. It was a real situation that we had the privilege to live through and I cannot help but remember it at this moment. When there is a will, when men are not discouraged, when they believe in what they are doing, no setback will make them back down!

As I said, our supplier was Batista's army, organized, equipped, trained and also advised during all that time by American officers. It was not an army to look down on, not at all. They believed themselves to be the masters of the world. We had to endure great needs but we gave our enemy prisoners our food and even our medicine.

We have the right to ask ourselves about that Serbia destroyed by NATO, if the West is going to refuse a handful of wheat to a pregnant woman in a country that is said to have surrendered and accepted every condition and still more conditions than those demanded by the Group of Eight? Is that correct? Is that fair? Is that humanitarian? I needed to ask those questions.

now here is the catch

I already told you that they were arguing over who was going to lead that security force. Of course, there is in the first place the speech delivered yesterday in the United Nations by the US ambassador. Actually, that Security Council agreement does not say under whose command the security forces are going to be. It only calls for them to go and it is known beforehand who can go and who will go.

Now the Yankees are interpreting the agreement. There comes the time for interpretations! This resolution establishes an international security force in Kosovo. Now here is the catch. In his speech, the United States representative says, among other things: 'The authorities of the Federal Republic of Yugoslavia accepted that KFOR,' I do not know how to pronounce it but that is the acronym – I do not know if it is in English or in what language – 'the Kosovo International Security Force will operate with a unified NATO chain of command,' this was just yesterday, after the resolution, 'under the political direction of the North Atlantic Council, in consultation with non-NATO force contributors.'

It is NATO and under the direction of the North Atlantic Council, in other words, the NATO Council. Who gave them permission? The Security Council? No. This demand was contained in the agreement of the Group of Eight meeting of May 6. Because, on May 6, when they saw that the bombings were continuing through March and all of April, forty-odd days had passed. Three days many times over and there was not the least sign of capitulation, they began to worry. Many of those in NATO began to make up things and they put up a Group of Eight meeting that took place on May 6, that is, 44 or 45 into the bombings, and they adopted certain agreements. The Russian prime minister had still not been changed but before that change took place somebody had been appointed as special envoy of the Russian government for the so-called peace efforts.

I am not criticizing that, of course. I think it was very appropriate that the Russian government did everything possible to try to find a political solution to the conflict. That conflict could not have a military solution and they were not in any condition nor they had any possibility to help the Serbs militarily, only with nuclear weapons and that is out of the question. Nobody would agree to that. That form of support would have seemed to us absolutely insane and impossible and it would have been a worldwide suicide.

But, it was obvious that the Russians did not even have the possibility of sending a plane with ammunition to Serbia. Nothing could be sent by land or sea. Hungary, a new NATO member is there on the border. There are other similar countries there. Nothing could be sent by land; nothing by air; nothing by sea. They had nothing but their nuclear weapons left and, let us say, political support, the firm denunciation of it all.

There was the Agreement of the Group of Eight under which a peace plan was adopted, a peace plan that after thorough discussions, was signed on May 6 and adopted or accepted by the Yugoslavs on June 3, that is, almost a month later. After its approval in May, many efforts were made: [President] Ahtisaari, from Finland, comes and goes, the same as Chernomyrdin. There were American envoys and Russian envoys until June 3, when during a visit to Belgrade the Russian envoy and the President of Finland convinced the President of Yugoslavia to accept the formula.

It has been said that the President of Finland went out and the Russian envoy once alone was finally able to convince the President of Yugoslavia. Some day we shall know what they said and how they said it. So, I am not criticizing the Russian peace efforts, that is quite different from the question of Yugoslav leaders accepting the conditions imposed on them. I have my personal view of the different things that might have happened. I will just say that in spite of its immense power, NATO's position was already weak because you cannot go on bombing and killing every day before the eyes of the whole world that is watching a live show of what is going on. There comes a moment when the killing becomes too scandalous and intolerable.

But nobody there talked about who was going to command the troops. That would be discussed later. Until the last minute, when the resolution was about to be submitted to the Security Council, the Russians opposed the idea that the troops taking part in the aggression be allowed there – that was also the Yugoslav position – and that there should be a single command under NATO. The mediators had to consult the Chinese, and the Chinese had reasons to be irritated by the method, the procedure used by NATO, the attack on the Chinese Embassy, all those things.

The Russians agreed to discuss the draft first in the Security Council and then discuss the organization and distribution modalities, the question of security forces in Kosovo. Giving in first to something and then discussing another important issue is not good tactics. You give in and when you start discussing then they ask for more. No, sir, take a few more minutes to get things straight before supporting the agreement, before renouncing the right to veto and voting in favour.

I know of Russian leaders who have made serious and honest efforts to find a solution to a really complicated and dangerous situation. They have weakened themselves a lot politically and people do not respect them like before. That is why nobody knew who was going to lead the troops.

But the Americans rapidly found a solution which is found in the speech delivered by the United States representative in the Security Council. Look, they were discussing in Macedonia with the representatives of the Serb troops in Kosovo. They discussed for a whole day but did not reach an agreement. They returned for a second day of discussions and used the situation to request a false permit. And now a new finding which was disclosed yesterday: the role of NATO had already been authorized.

It was not the Group of Eight or the United Nations or the Russians who agreed. They discussed with those Serb military chiefs in Macedonia and, according to them, the authorities of the Federal Republic of Yugoslavia accepted that KFOR operated with a unified NATO command under the political leadership of the North Atlantic Council, that is, the Yugoslavs gave them permission. There is evidence that they have made fools of the Russians. A cable revealing this was broadcast today showing that the Russians did not like it at all.

I am abusing your patience telling you a story but, after all, your presence here is voluntary while I have no other choice but to finish when I can, when I am through with what I have to say. Do not get any ideas, I do not make any extra money for this job which requires an effort. What I want to do, since they brought me here – it is your fault, I did not volunteer – is to complete the ideas I want to present which can be useful to our people, too. I cannot forget them, they would like to know many things and this is an opportunity to tell them although it might take some time.

They solved the problem. Who? The vanquished. Nobody else authorized the Americans and NATO and the British Generals who discussed with them, of course, following strict orders from Marshall Solana, with due respect to the new Minister of Foreign Affairs of Europe, the pre-united Europe. He is a pre-Minister of a supranational pre-authority. These are the tittles, more or less, strictly speaking.

Right away, the United Kingdom takes the floor and here is another underlined excerpt: 'The authorities of the Federal Republic of Yugoslavia and the Serb Parliament have now accepted the principles and demands set out in the G-8 statement of May 6 and in the Chernomyrdin–Ahtisaari paper.'

'This resolution and its annexes clearly set out the key demands of the international community.' They are the international community – NATO is – to which Belgrade must now oblige.

'They also provide for the deployment of an international civil presence, led by the United nations, and for an effective international security presence to re-establish a safe environment in Kosovo. . . . That is why NATO has made clear that it will be essential to have a unified chain of command under the political direction of the North Atlantic Council' – not the United Nations – 'in consultation with non-NATO force contributors. This force, with NATO at its core, will be commanded by a British General. The United Kingdom will provide the leading contribution, at least 13,000 troops.'

'To have come this far, to have secured Belgrade's acceptance of all our demands, required a huge diplomatic effort. My government pays tribute and expresses its gratitude to Mr. Chernomyrdin, President

Ahtisaari and Mr. Talbot for their outstanding contribution. The positive engagement of the Russian Government, via its Special Envoy and in the preparation of this Resolution by Ministers of the Group of Eight has been vital.' They start by saying that the Yugoslavs authorized NATO to lead the security forces.

Were the Russians happy? Ah, no! I did not bring that cable, unfortunately. But today there were news from Europe that a Russian force of about 500 paratroopers who were in Bosnia in over 20 armoured vehicles, trucks and some tanks moved forward, crossed over Serbia and were marching towards the Kosovo border to await there the entrance of different forces, that is, the solution of the problem of how forces were going to be distributed and, of course, they have said that Russian forces will not accept NATO command.

They must have been irritated when, without saying a word to anybody, 24 hours before the resolution and the American interpretations, they sent a column of paratroopers in armoured vehicles who have not crossed the border, so far. Undoubtedly, this is an answer to all these interpretations. They hate accepting the idea and I suppose that domestically, in their own country where all this has been very traumatic, it must be very difficult for the Russian leaders to accept that their troops there – whether they are 2,000, 4,000, 5,000, with or without a salary – be under NATO orders. It is only tricks and more tricks on the part of those who unleashed that dirty war. That is how it has all been.

These are the two main leaders, of course: the United States and the United Kingdom. They are also the two countries bombing Iraq every day. Nobody remembers this but it happens every day. It has become a habit, a daily shooting exercise to preserve their right to bomb every day. That is something they do on their own, and with all these problems nobody even remembers.

We had denounced that Yugoslavia had been turned into a shooting range. In a declaration on June 1st, that is, just nine days ago, before the government of Yugoslavia accepted the Group of Eight plan, Cuba issued a Declaration including different items. Among other things, reference was made to what was going on there day by day, each target, the attacks. That Declaration said, *inter alia*, 'Yugoslavia has become a military testing ground. Planes taking off from the United States drop their deadly load on the Serb people, refuel in midair and return to their bases non-stop. Missiles are air-launched at a distance off the range of anti-aircraft. Unmanned aircraft are bombing hospitals with patients inside, households with people inside, bridges full of pedestrians and buses with passengers.'

Anybody could say that it was an uncalled for denunciation on our part. But it so happens that yesterday – June 10, about nine days later – in Washington, a France Press cable by Benjamin Kahn, reported:

'NATO bombings in Yugoslavia against military targets and civil infrastructure allowed the US Air Force to test several high-tech weapons, upgraded since the 1991 Iraq War.

'Intelligent bombs designed to set their trajectory in flight were used in the Gulf War but the new upgraded versions were used in Yugoslavia and in a bigger number than ever before.

'Computer-guided bombs allowed the United States to kill thousands of Yugoslav soldiers from far away, without risking their pilots or ground troops.'

And it goes on:

'Analysts affirm that the massive use of new Cruiser missiles and other state-of-the-art weapons will continue growing as a result of the search of the US military to upgrade their capacity to attack beyond the reach of enemy defense.

'Another breakthrough since the Gulf War was the building-up of missiles' noses with titanium to allow them to run through thick layers of cement and explode causing greater damage.

'The new generation of B-2 Stealth bombers – the most expensive of all – also made their debut in Yugoslavia.

'At a cost a 2.2 billion dollars each, B-2s of a super-sophisticated technology, manufactured by Northrop Grumman, Boeing and General Electric, flew from a base in the state of Missouri and eluded the Yugoslav anti-aircraft defense and dropped many satellite-guided bombs in each flight.'

Today there are new facts. A dispatch reported that in three sorties such bombers hit 20 per cent of their targets; 20 per cent of the targets hit by bombs and missiles. They have been talking about that.

I believe that Mr Clinton went today to this air base to congratulate warmly and fraternally the super-heroes who, always out of reach of enemy weapons, killed hundreds or thousands of persons or caused who knows what sort of destruction. An exercise in new technology, and by air. They did not land midway. B-52s, flying straight from US territory, dropping tons and tons of bombs. They had to be tested using real fire against real targets.

the way they manipulate people with lies and demagogy

'Bombs dropped by B-2 JDAMs – also new – use a GPS orientation system weighing 450–900 kilos and costing 18,000 dollars each.' Rather cheap for an aircraft that, according to the Washington reporter, costs 2.2 billion. With 2.2 billion, according to the programmes I have been telling you about, you can estimate the hundreds of thousands of lives of children, and people in general, in Haiti, in Central America and similar places who could be saved in a few years. You can almost estimate how many lives can be saved in one year. This can be more than 400,000. Saving a child's life never costs more than 500 US dollars: from a child who dies for lack of a vaccine worth 25 cents to another who dies from lack of rehydration salts, etc. Let us say 500 US dollars, an exaggerated figure. With 500 million US dollars you could save almost 1 million people, if there are doctors and medicines.

With 1 billion US dollars, 2 million children can be saved; with 2 billion US dollars, 4 million children; with 2.2 billion US dollars, you could save the lives of 4.4 million children. Everyone knows, including the World Health Organization, that about 12 million children die of curable diseases, 10 to 12 million children. I do not recall exactly the latest figures.

Almost half of those dying in one year could be saved with the cost of a single aircraft. It would really be humanitarian to invest the cost of one of these planes in saving the lives of almost 4.5 million children by conservative estimates! Because in the programmes we are designing doctors work for free. We pay our doctors here, with our currency. We do not have to spend US dollars because they are paid in our own currency and recently all doctors wages have been raised. As for NATO it is surely setting a humanitarian record!

It is very sad the way they manipulate people with lies and demagogy. Actually, you should not leave without these few facts I still have here to share with you.

I say that there are three basic ideas. I have spoken of the Group of Eight. I already said who tabled the motion: seven out of 12 belonged to NATO, those I mentioned.

But, what is the Group of Eight? The Group of Eight is a company, a small club of the super-rich. On account of their major influence and money, the United States, Japan, Germany – tremendously rich countries – are there and all the others and they set monetary polices for the International Monetary Fund. They dictate measures for coping with crises and make certain arrangements if there is a crisis in Southeast Asia or in Russia or if there is any danger that it may spread to Latin America.

The Seven Rich meet annually. But with the collapse of the USSR and the improved relations with Russia, once in a while they invite it. From Russia alone, the West – mainly Europe – has taken out 300 billion US dollars. Of course, they did not go there to get them at gun-point. It was not necessary either because so skillful business people have cropped up there that they have become multimillionaires in a few years.

Under the reforms introduced by the West, Russia has suffered terribly. Its economy was cut by half; its defense considerably weakened. For granting her a 20 billion US dollar credit, the West imposes restrictions and demands many conditions that Russia cannot meet, some of them humiliating. What are 20 billion US dollars in Russia so badly in need after the August crisis? And spread throughout a whole year even if it is only one fifteenth of the hard currency that wound up in the West.

But not only that. The rouble has been devalued twice. Before, a rouble equalled a US dollar and had a higher purchasing power in Russia than a dollar. In a few years its purchasing power was 6 thousand times lower, that is, you needed 6 thousand roubles to buy 1 US dollar. All those who had savings, pensioners and others, lost them. As a result of devaluation, an entire nation lost its money.

They set a new parity and a new rouble. They took off the zeros, divided it by 1,000 and then, with 6 roubles you bought 1 dollar. Therefore, when the crisis began, those who had saved roubles found that their rubles instead of being rated 6 to 1 dollar were worth only 24 to 1 dollar, one fourth. Once again those with savings had lost their money. This has happened not only in Russia but in many other countries as well. Latin America is tired of living through these experiences, through the repeated devaluations I already mentioned. The currencies become volatile capital.

Where is the person who having lost all his savings in his own country twice would want to have his cash in the national currency again, even if it pays a 40, 50 or 80 percent interest rate. On the other hand, no economy can withstand that. It is impossible, because the mechanism recommended by the theoreticians of neo-liberalization in the International Monetary Fund to the countries is an increase in the interest rate, so that people do not take away their money. Which budget can withstand 80 per cent rates?

It is impossible. Besides, even if interest rates are raised to those levels, there can be a 400 to 500 per cent devaluation, incomparably higher than the increased rate. What do savers or people with revenues do? They exchange their money for dollars. No bank can resist that. How much money would a country need to keep the rouble–foreign exchange convertibility? An endless amount of dollars.

How many years will pass before the nationals of a country suffering this problem can have confidence in their currency again? And there goes the IMF demanding free conversion and lots of other unpractical things which cannot be implemented. A few estimates suffice to identify the problem, they change everything to dollars, stuff them inside a mattress and take them out of the country.

So the country is now very impoverished and heavily dependent on foreign credits. Yet, I do not believe it must necessarily be like that. A country like Cuba that has gone through a hard experience – without fuel, steel, lumber, anything and has survived without a dime from any international agency – knows that with its huge resources that country would not need any credits. As simple as that. I shall say no more. Just that if we had those resources we would be growing at a two digit rate. Without anything and despite everything, including the blockade, we are growing and this year we shall grow from 3 to 4 per cent, approximately.

We have the right to imagine what could be done. The revenues of most of our exports are spent just in fuel because the Revolution took electricity to the most distant places, to the mountains. 95 percent of the population has electricity although it was less than 50 per cent at the triumph of the Revolution, and oil was worth 7 US dollars a barrel and with 1 ton of sugar you could buy 7–8 tons of oil. Then, after the collapse of the socialist camp, oil prices climbed tremendously and with 1 ton of sugar we could only buy I ton of oil.

We do not have the immense Siberian forests, oil and gas fields.

We do not have a significant steel industry and machinery either. If we only had raw materials and today's experience, because we must add that we have learned to be more efficient and make a better use of our resources, the Cuban economy might grow perhaps 12 or 14 per cent.

It is my conviction, and this is the first time I say this in public, that that country can save itself. It does not have do depend on Western credits, sooner or later its leaders will understand that. But, undoubtedly, today it depends on credits.

I mentioned the Group of Eight. The seven richest countries in the world, six of them NATO members who unleashed and took an active part in that war, the other one is not a NATO member but is the main strategic ally of the United States in the Pacific: Japan. I do not intend to criticize Japan. We have good relations with that country. When we were hit by a hurricane after a severe drought, they spontaneously offered food relief to the most vulnerable populations worth 8 million US dollars, with which 30 thousand tons of rice were bought. That is a gesture we appreciate very much. I limit myself to the presentation of facts.

The group of the seven richest countries in the world except Japan, which is not a NATO member, took part in the attack on Serbia. The eighth country, Russia, is ironically the country that has become poorer in less time. Its per capita GDP is at Third World levels.

It is now an impoverished, indebted country depending on Western credits. Still, I am not suggesting at all that these were the reasons for the sad role it played in the Group of Eight. I believe that they were genuinely concerned about the crisis unleashed, the danger of this adventurous war and the impact on its own population, a mirror image of what might happen to them some day. They must have grown aware of all the influence and strength they have lost.

Actually, I would admit that their position is right in as much as they advocate a political solution of conflicts and the United Nations Charter. Their speech in the Security Council was critical and positive but, of course, that is the Group of Eight which was no longer inviting Russia but this time they called it, met with it and, it was in those circumstances that they participated.

I think it was this morning that I read some news on the rapid advance of a column of Russian paratroopers heading for Kosovo. It caught NATO by surprise; in fact, it caught everybody by surprise. It was an undeniable answer to the deceit of negotiating permission with the Yugoslavs so that NATO would head security forces in Kosovo. It was not a United Nations decision, it was not discussed with Russia. That was the humiliation, deceit and trickery.

In short, NATO attacked and got stuck. They invented a meeting of the Group of Eight and fabricated a peace plan. The peace plan which excited so many discrepancies and differences with the Russians was finally adopted and taken to the Security Council while the issue of who was in command of that force remained unresolved. But, the question had already been solved. Right there in his speech, the United States representative informed that they had permission from the Yugoslavs to take command of the Yugoslav province of Kosovo. That is the way the matter was handled. I think that everything is quite clear.

a holocaust, a true holocaust of a huge magnitude

I want to say something else. We started delving as deep as possible in the history of that region, its past and recent history, and we have put together some interesting information. There is one in particular, however, that has greatly struck our attention. It was denounced yesterday by our UN Ambassador: when Hitler invaded Yugoslavia he set up a fascist government in Zagreb which included Croatia, Bosnia, Herzegovina and a great part of Voivodina, almost to the doors of Belgrade.

The fascist regime of Ante Pavelic enforced the so-called Three-Thirds Doctrine. What did it mean? One-third of the Serbs were to be deported, another third assimilated and forcibly converted to Catholicism – the official religion of the country [Croatia] because the others, the Serbs, were Christians too but from another church, the Orthodox Church rather close, in general, to the Catholic doctrine although with evident tensions between them. The last third would be annihilated. That doctrine became the political orientation of the State machinery which started organizing all three things with unequally effective results.

Many of the converts were finally annihilated since deportation was not easy. Thus, physical extermination became the most general practice. Amazing! For us it was a discovery, a holocaust, a true holocaust of a huge magnitude.

In terms of the total Serb, not Yugoslav, population at that time it is possible that they annihilated (I only say that it is possible, because I still have not done the exact reckoning, someone should do it) a higher percentage of Serbs as compared to the total Serb population living in Croatia, Bosnia and Herzegovina than the percentage of Jews annihilated during World War II, *vis-à-vis* their total number. A more detailed study would be required. This holocaust has been hidden. The west never wanted to mention it.

We have tried to learn as much as possible about the authour of the research contained in this small book. He is a journalist who works with many humanitarian organizations. He was raised as a Catholic and not in the least close Marxism-Leninism or Communism. Looking for materials we found this. We are collecting more information. Some of his articles have been published and the book is certainly well written. It contains a lot of interesting data.

Now what do Croat and Serb writers say? Croat writers acknowledge that there were 200,000 victims, that is, those who were killed under the fascist Three-Thirds Doctrine. What do Serb writers say? They speak of 1 million people killed. What do more reliable sources say? That they were 400,000 to 700,000. What does one of the admittedly most reliable sources, the British Admiralty Archives, have to say? Do not forget that the United Kingdom was an ally of Yugoslavia at the time taking part in operations in the Balkans and their archives are considered important, serious sources. Raising the issue may perhaps awaken interest so that better informed people can speak up on it. The British Admiralty set 675,000 as the number of civilian Serbs killed, including many peasants and people of all ages and gender who were coldly murdered in concentration camps or in the places where they lived. Whole villages were wiped out. That was the figure used yesterday by our UN Ambassador. But there are other interesting data. I suspect the number of victims to have been higher.

There is a population analysis based on 1941 population data of three territories – Croatia, Bosnia and Herzegovina – their different cultures, ethnic groups and nationalities living there. Although among Bosnian-Herzegovinians, Serbs and Croats one cannot actually speak of ethnic differences because the three nations are ethnic Slavs. There is even a Serbo-Croatian language. The difference is rather cultural, religious and national. A single ethnic group may have several nations. In Latin America, besides the language we share many ethnic traits. The Dominican Republic and Cuba – just to mention an example – belong to the same ethnic group and are two independent nations.

According to statistics, in 1941 when there was still no war, how many Croats lived in that territory? In that territory the population was 3.3 million. Forty years later, according to the 1981 census, how many Croats were living there? 4,210,000, that is, an almost one million increase. Muslims, who are Slavs too but of the Muslim religion: in 1941, there were 700,000; in 1981, there were 1,629,000 (more than doubled). Serbs, how many Serbs were living in that same territory in 1941? 1,925,000. How many after 40 years, according to the 1981 census? 1,879,000, that is, approximately 45,000 less. Based on these facts, people who have analyzed population, customs, habits, growth, etc., have estimated that in that holocaust 800,000 to 900,000 Serbs died.

All of us have heard of Oswiecim and other concentration camps. Some of us have had the possibility of visiting them and having a terrifying vision of what those concentration camps were. Now we find out, or we are told, that there was an extermination camp called Jasenovac, the equal of Oswiecim in Poland. In Jasenovac lie the remains of hundreds of thousands of Serbs as well as thousands of Jews, gypsies and people of all ethnic groups. People say that the biggest Serbian city after Belgrade lies there, below the ground.

How many of you knew about it? Did anyone of you know or had anyone of you heard about this? We are going to keep on researching. Could you please raise your hand if you knew it. [*Somebody raises a hand*] Good, tell us. [*One of the delegates says that a book on this subject was published in Serbia and translated to several languages, but that in Europe people are generally ignorant of this Croat-Nazi–fascist alliance and the genocide they committed.*] Who wrote that book? [*He says that he believes it was written by two Serbs.*]

This one I have here, from which I took the information we are going to research deeper into – the fact that Croat writers themselves acknowledge the figure of 200,000, is significant – was written by Josep Palau, an ethnic Catalonian journalist. Since 1982 he has been involved in many international activities linked to European peace movements and has been a representative of various non-governmental organizations. He has also been a United Nations consultant.

I asked our ambassador in New York if he had any information because we had suggested to him to buy this book. [*Shows it.*] We sent him the references, but in a bookstore he was told that it would take six weeks to get it. Right away, yesterday, we e-mailed him a copy. He had the whole book there. Then he told me that he had read another very interesting article by the same author who is considered one of the most knowledgeable in the history of the Balkans and, in general, about these problems. We do not know anything else. That is why I asked, in case any of you knew.

It is understandable that Yugoslav leaders avoided digging into the issue. It is hard to do so when such a horrible thing has happened. When there have been century-old conflicts, undoubtedly digging into this type of problems would have run against the aim of building a solid federation, a united and just State, a peaceful society.

One could ask why the West does not speak of this holocaust. It is particularly important now when they have been dropping thousands and thousands of bombs on that same nation. To this we would have to add that these are only those who died in the territory of Croatia, Bosnia and Herzegovina because the fascist government imposed by Hitler covered more territory, including part of Voivodina. However, it seems that there is information only on the three aforementioned territories, not Voivodina.

We need to calculate the number of those who died in the territory ruled by that government and those who died in parts temporarily occupied by Italian fascists or Hungarian fascists.

The carnage must have ended by late 1942, because in 1943 there were many liberated territories, the guerrilla force was stronger. I will try to gather information to know what percentage of the population died in concentration camps at that time. I do not mean in combats, but in concentration camps, and killed in cold blood.

A holocaust and no one talks about it, why? There are sad and painful stories of the more recent massacres and ethnic cleansing, and I do not doubt that they did take place. I have not been there or seen it, nor am I going to ask for the papers. It is enough to know a bit about the history of hatred and real conflicts.

But I know, too, that during the 45 years that the Socialist Federal Republic of Yugoslavia existed, there was peace among all those ethnic groups. Tito himself was an ethnic Croat, but he knew how to win the love of the Serbs and the Serbs were actually the backbone of the resistance. It is understandable that in Tito's time there was not much talk about the matter. Today, in a split-up Yugoslavia and when in one part of the country a crime such as this has been committed, it is worthwhile making these truths known.

I must say that it is not my intention to incite or blame anybody, least of all the people in that country. I do not intend to blame the Croats for this. it would be like blaming the Germans for Hitler's massacres of Jews, gypsies and many others who died in concentration camps, in the systematic efforts to coldly exterminate an ethnic group, a nation, a multi-ethnic population or a single ethnic group.

But a holocaust of such magnitude is tremendously important. Blaming the Croat people would be like blaming the Italian people for the crimes of that clown named Mussolini. I cannot think of calling him anything else because that is what he was to a great extent and he killed many people, invaded, waged war, sent troops to the Soviet Union. It would be unfair to blame any people for the crimes committed by a fascist system. I want to make this clear, honestly. I am not blaming anybody, I simply rely on historical facts.

Something else must be said: the Jews who suffered the holocaust in Germany and elsewhere were very friendly to the Serbs and very grateful to them because the Serbs saved the lives of many Jews. It is even said that the US Secretary of State, on her way from Czechoslovakia sought refuge in Serbian territory and there she received help and support from the Serbs. They played a role, fighting heroically against Nazism. And I reiterate that our stance, the one we hold and shall hold, is based on principles.

we do not do things to make friends or enemies

If you have a chance, you can read the speeches delivered by our UN Ambassador. Our position on Kosovo is very clear there. Not only now, but 12 days after the bombings began, when as a direct or indirect consequence – surely, in my opinion, in the overwhelming majority of cases as a direct result – of the bombings, all sorts of conflicts must have triggered or worsened, we offered doctors to a religious Catholic community involved in assisting refugees. They told us about the tragedy there and we offered to send up to 1,000 doctors. Twelve days after the conflict began! This is not something new said a week before Cuba spoke in the United Nations. We did not say it publicly because we left it to them. Eventually, several weeks ago, we also said it publicly.

Likewise, when the Americans who occupy a base in our territory informed us – they usually do not do it – rather than request permission they informed that they would bring 20,000 Kosovars, in violation of the terms of the agreement under which they stay there, an agreement which has been violated by all possible means, but at least this time they had the decency of telling us, perhaps they thought that we would say that they should not bring the Kosovars. But we told them: 'We absolutely agree that you bring them. We are ready to cooperate in everything. We can offer our hospitals, water services, all the help we can give them.'

Later, perhaps they thought things over. Because it was really disgusting to unleash a war which, in its turn, would unleash a colossal migration, a human drama and bring those people from Albania to a naval base in a tropical country, a long distance away. I believe they finally brought 2,000 to a camp in their own territory. Out of the 1 million, with a generous and humanitarian spirit they have assisted a little over 2,000 refugees, Great Britain another handful, I believe that 0.8 per cent the two of them combined or some other rather negligible number of refugees.

We said that we agreed, that they would be welcomed in the occupied Cuban territory. We offered medical care and we reiterate it now. That was our clear and categorical position: respect for their cultural, national and religious rights and support for their autonomy. We went even further, and possibly many Yugoslavs do not understand this, or many Serbs do not understand this well, but we admitted the idea of independence provided all Kosovo ethnic groups attained a fair peace and the Serbs in other territories of that Republic reached an agreement peacefully and decided to do it. Yes, I say that it has to be peacefully and mutually agreed.

I believe that such a possibility exists. Yet, I do not think we should interfere with this delicate issue. We have stated our position. We have done our duty. We do not do things to make friends or enemies. Sometimes we hurt friends and make enemies at the same time. But there is something much more important than any temporary advantages: seriousness and honesty.

I have criticized the Europeans with the words I have used without having any feelings of animosity against them. But one day I will be able to demonstrate that I warned them very precisely, and only seven days after the attacks began, I warned them of what was going to happen exactly. I apologize for preserving and not declassifying this material.

One of the big European mistakes was that instead of working with moderate forces, they worked with the most extremist called by them fearful terrorists just a few months ago. It was only in 1998 that the movement went from a few hundred armed men to over 15,000 to 20,000 armed men. Now we have to find out what the famous CIA did, how many it trained, with which weaponry and what tasks it gave them. What nobody doubts is that this war practically had a time-table. I believe that the greatest chance for peace was in supporting moderate groups and not extremist groups, called terrorists shortly before. They use any term, any adjective.

This is the last idea I want to share, why should we be so concerned about this policy, this onslaught on sovereignty, this attempt to do away with the principles of the UN Charter? Why are all these theories invented, these doctrines I mentioned, so many pretexts for humanitarian intervention or against global threats? As I was saying, there is something called 'diplomacy supported by force' which is another concept. What else will follow?

We have had bitter experiences with the behaviour of US political leaders. Once in a while they elect someone with a religious ethic. I would dare mention a case in point: President James Carter. I cannot think of Carter waging this type of genocidal war. But we have known a few US presidents of whom the same cannot be said.

We have just sued the United States for 181 billion dollars, I already told you a bit about it. I hope they give you a copy of our legal demand. I think you had one in your briefcases, but just in case, for the benefit of those who have not read it since you have not had much time, I will brief you about it. In those pages there are two things, two major cases of cynicism described. In the lawsuit we said: 'The unquestionable historical truth about these events and the cynicism and lies that have invariably accompanied all American actions against Cuba can be found in the original documents of the time, produced by those who, from within that country, planned the policy of aggression and subversion against Cuba.'

The plots against Cuba and their actions began as soon as we passed a Land Reform Act because US companies here owned estates of 10,000, 50,000 and even 150,000 hectares. We passed a Land Act that logically and inevitably affected their properties and as of that moment, their crimes against Cuba began. By August the first terrorist actions were carried out, the first plans to assassinate Cuban leaders, and it was an honour that they devoted a good number of them to me. They started in November 1959. It is right there, in that same section.

Nobody here had spoken of socialism. We talked about socialism on April 16, when we buried the combatants who fell victims of the attacks by US warplanes manned by Cuban mercenaries and deceitfully carrying painted Cuban flags. They even had Stevenson say a big lie at the United Nations when he was an Ambassador, the same official explanation they gave when they said that they were rebel Cuban Air Force planes.

Actually, it served as a warning about something we were expecting. We foresaw an imminent mercenary landing in the attempt to destroy our small Air Force, which they were unable to because our fighter planes were scattered and the base was defended by anti-aircraft batteries. They destroyed part of it, but we still had more planes than pilots and the ones left operational were enough for the time the adventure lasted.

In one of its sections the lawsuit reads: 'In this token, it may be illustrative for this Court that, on March 17, 1960, at a meeting attended by Vice-President Richard Nixon,' – an angel – 'Secretary of Defence John N. Irwin, Under Secretary of State Christian Herter,' – who was later not elected president – 'Secretary of the Treasury Robert B. Anderson, Assistant Secretary of State Livingston T. Merchant, Assistant Secretary of State Roy Rubottom, Admiral Arleigh Burke of the Joint Chief of Staff, CIA Director Allen Dulles, the high-ranking CIA officers Richard Bissell and J.C. King and the White House officials Gordon Gray and General Andrew J. Goodpaster, the United States President approved the so-called "Program of Covert Action Against the Castro Regime"' – a number of brutal actions are mentioned before in the document – 'proposed by the CIA.'

'Among other things, that program enabled the creation of a secret intelligence and action organization within Cuba, for which the CIA allocated the necessary funds. In a recently declassified memorandum – they declassified it because almost 40 years have gone by, and it is a standard procedure – on that meeting, General Goodpaster noted: "The President"' – President Eisenhower – '"said that he knows of no better plan for dealing with this situation. The great problem is leakage and breach of security". Everyone must be prepared to swear that he [Eisenhower] has not heard of it. He said our hand should not show in anything that is done.'

Serious things were already taking place here. In August 1959 pirate attacks and bombings began, sugar cane fields were set on fire by planes coming from the United States and the ship *La Coubre* was blown up resulting in the death of 101 Cubans. The meeting had been held a few days before. Actually, that was a formal meeting, especially because the CIA had already suggested my assassination before the end of 1959, on December 11. Not even one year after the triumph of the Revolution! There are other more revolting things and they are here for those of you who have not read it.

This is another declassified document. Nixon was no longer Vice-President nor was Eisenhower President. Kennedy was President and it was after the Bay of Pigs invasion:

'On March 7, 1962, the Joint Chiefs of Staff stated in a secret document: . . . determination that a credible internal revolt is impossible of attainment during the next 9–10 months will require a decision by the United States to develop a Cuban "provocation" as justification for positive US military action.'

'On March 9, 1962, under the title *Pretexts to Justify US Military Intervention in Cuba*, the Office of the Secretary of Defence submitted to the Joint Chiefs of Staff a package of harassment measures aimed at creating conditions to justify a military intervention in Cuba'. See this? They were always looking for pretexts. Some of the measures considered included the following, which were taken to the Joint Chiefs of Staff by the Office of the Secretary of Defence:

'A series of well coordinated incidents will be planned to take place in and around Guantanamo [Naval base] to give a genuine appearance of being done by hostile Cuban forces', one of their alternatives.

'The United States would respond by executing offensive operations to secure water and power supplies, destroying artillery and mortar emplacements threatening the base. Commence large-scale United States military operations.

'A "Remember the Maine" incident could be arranged in several forms.

'We could blow up a US ship in Guantanamo Bay and blame Cuba.

'We could blow up a drone [unmanned] vessel anywhere in the Cuban waters.

'We could arrange to cause such incident in the vicinity of Havana or Santiago as a spectacular result of a Cuban attack from the air or sea, or both.

'The presence of Cuban planes or ships merely investigating the intent of the vessel could be fairly compelling evidence that the ship was taken under attack.

'The US could follow up with an air/sea rescue operation covered by US fighters to "evacuate" remaining members of the non-existent crew.

'Casualty lists in US newspapers would cause a helpful wave of national indignation.

'We could develop a Communist-Cuban terror campaign in the Miami area, in other Florida cities and even in Washington. The terror campaign could be pointed at Cuban refugees seeking haven in the United States.

'We could sink a boatload of Cubans en route to Florida (real or simulate).

'We could foster attempts on lives of Cuban refugees in the United States even to the extent of wounding in instances to be widely publicized.

'Exploding a few plastic bombs in carefully chosen spots, the arrest of Cuban agents and the release of prepared documents substantiating Cuban involvement would also be helpful in projecting the idea of an irresponsible government.

'A "Cuban-based, Castro-supported" filibuster could be simulated against a neighbouring Caribbean nation.

'Use of MIG-type aircraft by US pilots could provide additional provocation.

'Harassment of civil aircraft, attacks on surface shipping and destruction of US military drone aircraft by MIG-type planes would be useful as complementary actions.

'An F-86 properly painted would convince air passengers that they saw a Cuban MIG, especially if the pilot of the transport were to announce such fact.

'Hijacking attempts against civil air and surface craft should appear to continue as harassing measures condoned by the government of Cuba.

'It is possible to create an incident which will demonstrate convincingly that a Cuban aircraft has attacked and shot down a chartered civil airliner en route from the United States to Jamaica, Guatemala, Panama or Venezuela.

'The passengers could be a group of college students off on a holiday or any grouping of persons with a common interest to support chartering a non-scheduled flight.

'It is possible to create an incident which will make it appear that Communist-Cuban MIGs have destroyed a USAF aircraft over international waters in an unprovoked attack'.

'Five months later' – of these sinister, truly sinister variables suggested by the Joint Chiefs of Staff – 'in August 1962' – mark the year – 'General Maxwell D. Taylor, chairman of the Joint Chiefs of Staff, confirmed to President Kennedy that no possibility was perceived whereby the Cuban government could be overthrown without direct US military intervention, which was why the Special Group-Augmented was recommending the even more aggressive approach of Operation Mongoose. Kennedy authorized its implementation: "It's a matter of urgency".'

we carried out the cheapest revolution ever

1962: October [Missile] Crisis. Some news simply came to the Soviets' attention and to our attention. Not this document I just read, at least, we did not know about it.

But Khrushchev was totally convinced. For us it was something we were used to. We were always mobilized on news of a possible invasion. We were not interested in having strategic missiles here. Actually, we were more interested in the image of our country, that it would not look like a base of our Soviet friends.

The decision was made based on our sense of solidarity because before the Bay of Pigs invasion they had sent us many weapons. We had hundreds of thousands of weapons. We had already bought them from the socialist camp and the USSR since that March 4 when *La Coubre* was blown up. It was in 1960, she was bringing weapons from Belgium. The rest of the time until the Bay of Pigs invasion in April, that is, 1 year and 1 month later, we received dozens and dozens of ships with weapons from the USSR through Czechoslovakia: tanks and cannons, anti-aircraft artillery and rifles.

Very soon we learned how to use them because the heaviest got here during the first quarter of 1960, and when the Bay of Pigs invasion was launched, we had weapons taken from Batista's army and some we had bought in Belgium – the second cargo was the one blown up. We did not want to give them any excuse, as in the case of Guatemala where they had used the pretext of a ship carrying weapons from Czechoslovakia to Arbenz's government and blown up the ship. But, by the time of the invasion, we had hundreds of thousands of men trained and armed, thousands and thousands of artillery men to operate those weapons. They were not very experienced, but they could handle those weapons and had a fighting spirit.

The Soviets were very, very concerned because they got news of a possible invasion. They gave us the sources, not the most important, not tome. The information they possibly received was incomplete but they did give us the information they extracted from their talks with Kennedy and other high-ranking personalities.

By the time of Bay of Pigs invasion they had sent us not only weapons, but they had also made very strong statements and even spoken of the missiles. They were irritated because at that time the Cuban Revolution was like a miracle. They could not have imagined it. It was not imported or promoted by anyone from abroad. It was truly and fully ours.

The only thing we imported, actually, were the ideas, or rather, the books from which we got a revolutionary political culture. To this we added some Cuban notions and tailored it to the Cuban reality. According to Engels – I must say this – ever since the big avenues were built in Paris and a rifle firing five bullets was invented, he considered that from that moment onwards an uprising in Paris or similar places would be impossible.

We had to build our revolutionary consciousness when there were planes, tanks, cannons, communications and many things unimaginable in Engels' days. Since we believed in a number of principles and had a tradition, we conceived the idea of an armed struggle, the strategy and tactics to be pursued.

No Russian had absolutely anything to do with it. No Soviet. Nobody. Nobody sent us guns either. Nobody gave us a dime. Later, there were revolutionary movements in this hemisphere that had tens of millions of dollars. One day I estimated the cost of the Moncada, the Granma and the Sierra Maestra warfare; perhaps I am not too wrong if I put their cost at 300,000 US dollars. So, we can score another point to our favour and say that we carried out the cheapest revolution ever.

I am being very candid with you. Yes, we have stood in solidarity with the revolutionary movement. We have not denied it. We may not tell the enemy what we do not want it to know, but we never tell lies. That is for sure, we never tell lies to them, to journalists or to anybody. That is an invariable principle.

I was telling you about the [Missile] Crisis. We knew that the Americans had some missiles in Turkey and Italy, medium-range missiles which are faster than strategic missiles and bombers. There is no doubt that the presence of 42 missiles here gave the Soviets a certain strategic balance. So, for us, who received weapons, support and even the hope that they might fight for us, no matter how much we wanted to preserve a certain image of the Revolution, it was not fair, it was not honourable to refuse an agreement on the question of medium-range missiles. Actually, for us it would have been better to run the risk of not having them, although based on what we know today, the invasion was a sure thing.

By that time, the number of weapons and trained people we had was considerable. We would have been a Vietnam and paid a very high price.

Why did the attack not take place? The Soviet thesis proved its value. We received additional news, but we did not pay attention because we were used to such hazards. We had no fear of imperialism or anything like it and we had the experience of our war which was short but intense, therefore, it was the best of schools to enrich that experience. The Soviets were fully convinced, a conviction that could not come out of the blue, without access to documents or other sensitive sources of information.

Looking back at those times, I see that the recommendations to fabricate a pretext date from March 9, 1962.

It is known that the Soviets had some friends or sympathizers in many US institutions taking part in meetings with a lot of people, meetings resulting in lots of papers. They had them. At that time, as I said, we did not know of these documents. But, carefully recalling the story of the contacts, the first time they told us about it, the envoys that came to Cuba, who they were and what they talked about, what they said and how they said it, and the way in which we analyzed it, I do not have any doubts that what they knew came from very reliable sources. I discussed the problem with the revolutionary leadership. In those days Che, Raul and other comrades were the main leaders; we analyzed it and made a decision.

The Soviets asked me a question, I should say it. They asked me: 'What do you think would prevent this invasion?' I told them, and I still believe it: 'A Soviet declaration stating that an attack on Cuba would be tantamount to an attack on the Soviet Union.' They said: 'Yes, yes. But how do we make it plausible?' That was when they suggested deploying the missiles. Then we started thinking and analyzing among ourselves, and we analyzed it from the angle I told you, in terms of honour and solidarity. The answer was 'Yes'. That was weeks after instructions had been given to fabricate the pretext for an invasion.

I have to reconstruct that story a bit, inquire about some facts and dates. I already told you about this – I was only going to read what I had here – and be more precise. Because the moment we signed an agreement on that, we began working really fast. So, by August Kennedy had accepted the plan, adopted the plan and said: 'It's a matter of urgency.'

We probably prevented a direct invasion at that time. Later, there were rumours of movements of arms and ships, and so on. In July and August there were some rumours because the missiles were arriving – land-to-air missiles – and a large amount of weapons, modern planes and many other things. The Crisis began after October 20, really. The Soviets were absolutely right. Khrushchev was absolutely right. But such certainty as he had would not have been possible without access to the documents and activities in which the Unites States was engaged. And they had many more resources than we did to obtain that information.

We had some hard information, enough I think and, above all, intuition; we outguessed them. On the other hand, we had a rule: An attack should never take us by surprise. It is better to mobilize twenty times, even if nothing happens, than not mobilizing once and be attacked. We might say that a mobilized troop or country is 20–25 times stronger than when taken by surprise.

That was what happened to the Soviets in June 1941. That happened to Stalin, when he behaved like an ostrich, sticking his head into a hole while the Germans concentrated 3 million troops near the border, tens of thousands of vehicles, thousands upon thousands of tanks, thousands upon thousands of planes. They attacked on a Sunday, when many officers and soldiers were on leave and they destroyed almost every plane on the ground. That story is incredible and we know it very well because we have read a lot about that war and it has helped enrich our experience in many fields.

It was only when the Americans decided to declassify these documents that we learned the details of those sinister plans and their unbelievable lack of scruples. One of those people said: 'I don't know anything. You must be prepared to swear that I don't know anything about it.' Another one recommended shameful ways to fabricate pretexts to justify a war. The other one accepted. All this is useful today. Other documents will be declassified because there is this procedure, and that has been a contribution – as I was saying – the declassified documents, in addition to all the evidence we have. Something like the Bay of Pigs is definitely easy to prove. But there is a whole story, from the first to the last man recruited, who did it, where he was sent, the weapons he was given. We took 1,200 prisoners here and swapped them for baby food and medicine. That was the compensation they paid.

Through the declassification process they have put in our hands documents, precedents and facts. Now, we are engaged in this legal battle. I hope that they do not invade us because they consider it a global threat.

those are indeed global threats:
speaking, reasoning, thinking, explaining, showing

I can certainly speak of another global threat, namely, ideas. Clear ideas, all that you have analysed and adopted. We should all help globalize ideas, help them expand. We should all work the miracle of sending them everywhere, as I said the first day. Those are indeed global threats: speaking, reasoning, thinking, explaining, showing. If in your opinion I have been too extensive, in my opinion I have not.

It has been a pleasant experience to discuss all this with you, and I have told you a number of things, many of which I have exposed for the first time. I have done it with great pleasure, with great satisfaction. It is

the least I can do for the honor of your visit, because you have come without
any fears and under certain circumstances you need to be brave to come
and visit us. I am talking to the Congress delegates. I am talking, too –
although it is not the same situation – to the Ministers. Ministers are more
powerful, therefore, less vulnerable than you.

For the spirit of friendship we have seen, for your honesty and
solidarity it has been a great satisfaction to speak to you for I do not know
how many hours – I can hardly estimate the number – but I can assure
you that if I started talking at 5.00 p.m., it is still far from the record. I
hope it can be useful!

Thank you.